# SUPPORTING CAPITAL MARKET DEVELOPMENT AND REFORM IN DEVELOPING ASIA

## COUNTRY ASSESSMENT REPORT FOR AZERBAIJAN

APRIL 2026

ASIAN DEVELOPMENT BANK

ADB

6 ADB Avenue, Mandaluyong City, 1550 Metro Manila, Philippines
Tel +63 2 8632 4444; Fax +63 2 8636 2444
www.adb.org



ISBN 978-92-9277-767-8 (print); 978-92-9277-768-5 (PDF); 978-92-9277-769-2 (ebook)
Publication Stock No. SPR260138-2
DOI: http://dx.doi.org/10.22617/SPR260138-2



Notes:
In this publication, "$" refers to United States dollars.
ADB recognizes "Korea" as the Republic of Korea.

Cover design by Cleone Flores Baradas.
On the cover, clockwise from top left (i) photo of railway construction from Poyle to Salakhle, (ii) urban landscape of Türkiye, (iii) construction of power facility in Azerbaijan, (iv) stacks of coins, (iv) city view of Azerbaijan, (vi) graph showing upward trend.

# CONTENTS

# TABLES, FIGURES, AND BOXES

## Tables



## Figures



## Boxes

# ACKNOWLEDGMENTS

This publication was prepared as part of the technical assistance for the project on Supporting Capital Market Development and Reform in Developing Asia (Phase 1), executed by the Asian Development Bank (ADB).

It was produced by a team of consultants comprising Beop-Yong Jeon, primary author and expert in payment, clearing, and settlement systems; Yoonhee Kim, director, International Finance Division, Korea Financial Services Commission and former financial sector specialist, Financial Sector Office, Sectors Group, ADB; Ki-Hoon Ro, financial market infrastructure expert; Pilkyu Kim, senior research fellow, Korea Capital Market Institute; and Laila Catherina Q. Deles, research assistant, ADB.

Kyungsoo Shin, head of treasury team, Kookmin Bank London Branch and former financial sector specialist, Finance Sector Office, Sectors Department 3 (SD3-FIN), led the efforts to coordinate and contribute to the development and production of the publication. The publication was reviewed by Samir Ismayilov, financial sector specialist, SD3-FIN; and Sanan Shabanov, senior private sector development officer, Azerbaijan Resident Mission.

The publication has benefited from the comments of Esli Dilbazi, director, Financial Services and Settlement Department, National Depository Center of the Republic of Azerbaijan; Paul G.C. Lee, capital markets reform expert; Chul Kim, director of Payment System Policy Division, Bank of Korea; Yong-Gu Kim, head of BOK-Wire Operations Team, Bank of Korea; Gyung-Su Jang, head of Payment System Risk Management Team, Bank of Korea; and Dr. In-Ug Ryu, Korea Exchange (retired). The team wishes to express its great appreciation to these experts for their generous contributions of time and their insightful comments.

The publication was produced with the support of Katherine Mitzi Co, operations analyst, SD3-FIN. Consultant Ma. Kristina Mahilum provided valuable administrative support.

This publication does not represent the official views of ADB or any of the institutions mentioned herein.

# ABBREVIATIONS

| | |
|---|---|
| BSE | Baku Stock Exchange |
| CBA | Central Bank of the Republic of Azerbaijan |
| CCP | central counterparty |
| CPMI | Committee on Payments and Market Infrastructures |
| CSD | Central Securities Depository |
| DVP | delivery versus payment |
| FMI | financial market infrastructure |
| IC | investment company |
| IOSCO | International Organization of Securities Commissions |
| KC | key consideration |
| NDC | National Depository Center |
| OTC | over-the-counter market |
| PFMI | Principles for Financial Market Infrastructures |
| Pr. | Principle |
| SSS | securities settlement system |

# 1 INTRODUCTION

## Background

In response to a request from the Central Bank of the Republic of Azerbaijan (CBA), the knowledge and support technical assistance (TA) on Supporting Capital Market Development and Reform in Developing Asia (Phase 1) identifies gaps and recommends actions for the National Depository Center (NDC) to implement its new operations as the settlement agent in Azerbaijan.

Under the amendment to the Republic of Azerbaijan Law on Securities Market passed in July 2023, the NDC was granted the right to provide limited banking services in assuming the role of a settlement agent—a function currently performed by existing commercial banks.

Consequently, the NDC can provide clearing and settlement services not only for existing securities accounts but also for newly opened cash accounts. The NDC is exempted from having to obtain an appropriate license to engage in the following activities:

(i) opening and maintaining cash accounts for investment companies, banks providing investment services, issuers of publicly offered investment securities, depositories of investment funds, managers of investment funds, and nominal custodians[1] (Article 17.2.1.1); and

(ii) providing clearing and settlement services for cash accounts (Article 17.2.1.2).[2]

The NDC may provide settlement agent services in line with the above regulations (i) and (ii).[3] The questions addressed in this paper are motivated by the amendment to the law, which has paved the way for new business roles for the NDC. The TA assesses the issues likely to affect the

1 Nominal custodian refers to the legal and natural persons of foreign states that must submit information about financial transactions to the authorities of those foreign states.

2 The NDC is allowed to conduct investment fund depository activities (Article 17.2). An investment fund is a financial institution, created in the form of a joint-stock or shared investment fund, which engages in investing funds in the manner stipulated in the investment declaration, with the purpose of attracting funds and making profits. This report excludes consideration of this business, but it will be addressed in the consultation.

3 The current *Joint Agreement on Clearing and Settlement of Securities and Derivatives* should be revised to designate the NDC as the settlement agent.

NDC's execution of its new roles, with particular attention to ensuring that clearing and settlement arrangements are safe and efficient, in line with international standards. This publication is based on consultation with the NDC concerning its rules and regulations, discussions of the model-to-be, and reference models. It focuses on issues involved in the performance of securities clearing and settlement by the settlement agent, such as credit and liquidity risk, collateral, and default management. Issues for consideration are identified to plan robust settlement agent services by the NDC, to enhance central banking services to the financial market infrastructure, to improve credit and liquidity risk management based on the current guarantee mechanism, and to introduce central counterparty (CCP) functionality. These will feed into the country assessment report for Azerbaijan under the TA (forthcoming).

## Definitions: Settlement Bank and Settlement Agent in Azerbaijan

According to the Committee on Payments and Market Infrastructures (CPMI) of the Bank for International Settlements, *settlement*, *settlement bank*, and *settlement agent* are defined as follows:[4]

- **Settlement.** "The completion of a transaction, wherein the seller transfers securities or financial instruments to the buyer, and the buyer transfers money to the seller. A settlement may be final or provisional."
- **Final settlement.** "The discharge of an obligation by a transfer of funds and a transfer of securities that have become irrevocable and unconditional."
- **Settlement agent.** "An institution that manages the settlement process (e.g., the determination of settlement positions, monitoring of the exchange of payments, etc.) for transfer systems or other arrangements that require settlement."[5]
- **Settlement bank.**[6] "Either a central bank or private bank used to effect money settlements; the entity that maintains accounts for the settlement agent in order to settle payment obligations arising from securities transfers, both on its own behalf and for other market participants."

In Azerbaijan, the entities designated as settlement agents and settlement banks differ between the exchange and the over-the-counter (OTC) markets.

### 1. Exchange Market

The CBA is the settlement bank that renders settlement services for settlement agents to fulfill their cash obligations arising from transactions on the Baku Stock Exchange (BSE).

4 Committee on Payments and Market Infrastructures (CPMI). 2016. *A Glossary of Terms Used in Payments and Settlement Systems.*

5 The settlement agent's role can also be undertaken by a (usually not-for-profit) company or organization owned by the members of the central bank's large-value payment system. Given its generic function of safekeeping and administering securities for its customers, a custodian (often a bank) may also provide settlement agent services. It may also provide various other services, including clearing and settlement, cash management, foreign exchange, and securities lending.

6 Committee on Payment and Settlement Systems. 2003. *The Role of Central Bank Money in Payment Systems.* "Payments between banks are made by exchanging the liabilities of this settlement institution (the settlement asset)."

The settlement agent model is regulated by the *Joint Agreement on Clearing and Settlement of Securities and Derivatives* among the CBA, the NDC, the settlement agents, and the investment companies. The agreement defines settlement agents as "banks that are members of the Azerbaijan Interbank Payment System operating in the Republic of Azerbaijan, which determine the trading limits for conducting transactions on the BSE by investment companies and execute the monetary obligations arising from the transactions concluded by the investment companies in the amounts of those limits." A trading limit refers to "the monetary limit set by the settlement agent to the investment company for the purchase of securities and derivative financial instruments on the stock exchange during one trading day, including securities subject to repo/reverse-repo transactions." As of December 2025, nine commercial banks served as settlement agents, and 12 investment companies maintained contractual relationships with them.

The functions of a settlement agent are summarized as follows:[7]

- providing trading limits to the investment companies with which the settlement agent cooperates on a contractual basis,
- opening accounts for investment companies,
- executing the cash payments of investment companies,
- opening temporary accounts for securities issuers.[8]

## 2. Over-the-Counter Market

Corporate bonds and shares can be traded on the OTC market. Transactions are executed through investment companies and public notaries. Unlike on-exchange transactions, OTC transactions are not settled through a settlement agent-guaranteed way. The cash legs of transactions are settled on a free-of-payment basis,[9] which is not a delivery-versus-payment mode. However, settlement risk is managed. Once the document confirming the payment order is presented to the NDC, the securities are transferred there. The cash leg is settled into any bank account agreed upon by the transacting parties.[10]

7 From the *Membership to Settlement Agent Model* on the NDC website.
8 These are escrow accounts, which are used for coupon payments or other corporate action-related payments.
9 This refers to a transfer of securities without a corresponding transfer of funds.
10 The investment company or client presents the document confirming the payment order to the NDC.

# 2 SCOPE AND METHODOLOGY

## Overview

The scope of this publication is the NDC's settlement agent function, mainly associated with bond transactions and settlements, with a focus on the secondary market, which is more relevant to market transactions than the primary market. Larger principal and liquidity risks can be created in the secondary market than in the primary market, where an official agent is involved in the typical government bond issuance process. In Azerbaijan, the delivery-versus-payment (DVP) scheme is said to to be in place, as detailed in Box 1. The securities purchased and the funds used to pay for them are exchanged simultaneously to eliminate securities settlement risk.

The key feature of securities settlement in Azerbaijan is that the settlement agent guarantees the settlement of on-exchange securities transactions conducted by investment companies. A settlement guarantee exists—in the case where the settlement agent ensures that cash settlement will be completed—by imposing a trading limit backed by pre-deposited assets, such as funds transferred (prefunded cash), financial pledges, bank guarantees, and insurance contracts. "In markets where a CCP does not exist, a guarantee arrangement may provide market participants with some degree of protection against losses from counterparty defaults."[11]

At present, this guaranteed model is being adopted for Azerbaijani securities settlement.[12] Payment on behalf of the investment company is guaranteed by the settlement agent. Notably, DVP1 transactions are also guaranteed for settlement by the settlement agent. The use of DVP2 is not regarded as a disputable issue. As the cash leg is net settled in the DVP2 model (Box 2), its settlement risk must be fully covered by sufficient financial resources. This paper identifies the potential risk factors based on an assessment of the "model-to-be." This is the case with the NDC assuming the role of settlement agent, as described in section III.

11 "Such arrangements are typically organized and managed by the [central securities depository] or [securities settlement system] for a market, or by some other market operator. A guarantee is typically viewed as desirable, or even necessary, where market rules or other features make it practically impossible for market participants to manage their counterparty credit risks bilaterally. Guarantee arrangements vary greatly, from simple insurance-based schemes to more sophisticated structures comparable to a CCP." Committee on Payments and Market Infrastructures and International Organization of Securities Commissions (CPMI-IOSCO). *Principles for Financial Market Infrastructures*, p. 9, footnote 11.

12 The World Bank (2006) also mentions that "counterparty risk exposure between participants is low, as the Baku Stock Exchange provides almost simultaneous settlement involving the pre-funding of cash and deposit of securities prior to trade." World Bank. 2006. *Payments and Securities Clearance and Settlement Systems in Azerbaijan*, p. 47.

## Box 1: Delivery Versus Payment Scheme in Azerbaijan

In delivery versus payment (DVP), Model 1, both securities and funds are typically settled on a gross basis. In DVP Model 2, in contrast, the securities are typically settled on a gross basis, with final transfer of securities from the seller to the buyer occurring throughout the processing cycle, while the funds are settled on a net basis.[a]

For DVP2 in Azerbaijan, funds are transferred after multilateral netting, and securities—which are blocked at the trading stage—are delivered via a gross mode simultaneously once a day at 2 p.m.

The settlement cycle refers to the time it takes to complete a securities transaction from the point of trade execution to the actual transfer of securities and cash between the parties involved. In Azerbaijan, final settlement occurs no later than T+1.

The table lists DVP schemes and settlement cycles for the respective bond products.

### DVP Models and Settlement Cycles, by Bond Product

| | Primary Market | Secondary Market | Repos |
|---|---|---|---|
| DVP1 | Notes of central bank (T+0) | Notes of central bank (T+0) | First leg (Repo) (T+0), Second leg (Reverse-repo) |
| | Corporate bonds (T+0) | Government bonds (T+0) | |
| | Shares (T+0) | | |
| DVP2 | Government bonds (T+1) | Corporate bonds (T+1) | - |
| | | Shares (T+1) | |

a Committee on Payments and Market Infrastructures. 2016. *A Glossary of Terms Used in Payments and Settlement Systems.*

Source: National Depository Center.

## Box 2: Delivery Versus Payment Model 2 or 3 Mechanism with Guarantee

A securities settlement system that uses a delivery versus payment Model 2 or 3 mechanism and explicitly guarantees settlement, whether the guarantee is from the financial market infrastructure itself or from its participants, should maintain sufficient financial resources to fully cover, with a high degree of confidence, all current and potential future exposures using collateral and other equivalent financial resources.

Source: Committee on Payments and Market Infrastructures and International Organization of Securities Commissions (CPMI-IOSCO). 2012. *Principles for Financial Market Infrastructures*, Explanatory Note (KC) 3.4.13, Principle 4.

This analysis presents two options as potential replacements for the current model, the "baseline" and the "recommended" models, based on the following criteria (outlined in Table 1):

(i) the guarantor,
(ii) the types of guarantee, and
(iii) the guarantor's access to liquidity in preparation for any payment default by a participating institution.

**Current model.** Banks act as settlement agents, receiving four types of guarantees from investment companies to specify their limits. Within these limits, the settlement agent guarantees investment company securities settlements through the DVP1 and DVP2 mechanisms (As-Is: Current Model). In case of an investment company's default, the settlement agent, as per a prearranged agreement, acts to fulfill the investment company's payment obligations. The settlement agent is a credit institution eligible for central bank loans.

**Baseline model.** The NDC is assumed to replace the existing eight settlement agents and take over their functions. The NDC receives four types of guarantees from an investment company to assign limits, within which it acts as a settlement agent for the investment company's securities settlements using DVP2 mechanisms (To-Be [1]: Baseline Model). To prepare for the possibility of payment defaults by banks or investment companies in DVP2 settlements, the NDC should source liquidity from commercial banks or central bank. In the event of a payment default in DVP2 settlements, the NDC should secure a credit line from a commercial bank to fulfill its settlement guarantee. This model also assumes that the NDC can establish a clearing fund—a kind of loss-sharing fund—to prepare for any member default.

A DVP1 transaction assumes a gross settlement method, where each participant is responsible for settling its own transactions without any guarantee. For DVP1 transactions, the CBA is assumed to provide liquidity to participants through an intraday repo arrangement (Central Bank's Intraday Liquidity Provision) or another method, such as an intraday overdraft.

**Recommended model.** Here, the NDC is endowed with CCP functionality, allowing it to assume the rights and obligations of the clearing member and guarantee the settlement of transactions.[13]

The difference between the current model and the baseline model is that the NDC alone performs the guarantee role in the baseline model, along with the trading limit setting that was previously undertaken by the eight settlement agents.

The difference between the baseline model and the recommended model is that the baseline model ensures contract performance.

13 For DVP1 transactions, two options are assumed to be available: (i) settlement can occur on an unguaranteed basis, with each market participant taking responsibility for its own transactions; and (ii) the CCP can conduct a clearing arrangement.

## Table 1: Current and Potential Settlement Agent Models

| | | Current Model | Baseline Model | Recommended Model |
|---|---|---|---|---|
| **1. Basis** | Law | Law on Payment Services and Payment Systems[a] | Law on Securities Market | To be reviewed |
| | Joint Agreement | Among CBA, NDC, banks, and investment companies | To be updated | To be abolished |
| **2. Settlement Agent** | | Banks | NDC | NDC as CCP |
| **3. Guarantor for payment in cash-leg** | DVP 1 | Settlement Agent | Buyer's responsibility | Buyer's responsibility/NDC |
| | DVP 2 | Settlement Agent | NDC | NDC |
| **4. Types of guarantees** | | (i) Cash<br>(ii) Cash or securities under financial pledges<br>(iii) Bank guarantees<br>(iv) Insurance contracts | (i) Cash<br>(ii) Cash or securities under financial pledges<br>• Mark-to-market valuation<br>• Haircut for each asset category<br>(iii) Bank committed credit lines<br>(iv) Bank guarantees<br>(v) Insurance contracts | CCP waterfall structure<br>(i) Defaulter's margin<br>(ii) Defaulter's contribution to the default fund<br>(iii) CCP's skin-in-the-game (CCP's reserves)<br>(iv) Non-defaulter's contribution to the default fund<br>(v) CCP's additional reserves |
| **5. Guarantor's access to liquidity** | DVP 1 | Settlement agent refinanced by CBA[b] | Intraday repos/overdrafts between NDC (or bank/investment company) and CBA[c] against securities on flow/self-collateralization (government bonds and CBA notes) | Intraday repos/overdrafts between NDC (or bank/investment company) and CBA[c] against securities on flow/self-collateralization (government bonds and CBA notes) |
| | DVP 2 | | Credit lines from banks | Credit lines from banks |
| **6. Buyer's nonfulfillment of payment within the day** | DVP 1 | Settlement agent is responsible for the payment obligation as a guarantor | (i) CBA's selling of securities under prior agreements<br>(ii) In case of no potential buyers, CBA deals with default in terms of rules on repo or other lending procedures[d] | (i) CBA's sale of securities under prior agreements<br>(ii) In case of no potential buyers, CBA deals with default in terms of rules on repo procedures[d] |
| | DVP 2 | | (i) Committed credit lines from commercial banks pledging collateral<br>(ii) Loss sharing | (i) CCP ensures settlement by activating CCP risk management<br>(ii) Committed credit lines from commercial banks |

CBA = Central Bank of the Republic of Azerbaijan, CCP = central counterparty, DVP = delivery versus payment, NDC = National Depository Center.

[a] Article 45.

[b] Law on the Central Bank of the Republic of Azerbaijan, Article 33.

[c] Adopting an appropriate model in accordance with the monetary policy framework of the CBA.

[d] When the trading institution fails to make the payment or deliver the securities on the redemption date in the repo trading, the specified securities may be disposed of at the discretion of the CBA. The CBA may impose sanctions, such as suspension of trading eligibility.

Source: Author.

The NDC case was reviewed against the *Principles for Financial Market Infrastructures* (PFMI) and the assessment methodology of the Committee on Payments and Market Infrastructures-Technical Committee of the International Organization of Securities Commissions (CPMI-IOSCO).[14] The focus is on the NDC's role in its money and securities settlement function. Thus, the referenced PFMIs mainly concern (i) credit and liquidity risk management (principles 4–7), (ii) settlement (principles 8–9), (iii) central securities depositories and exchange-of-value settlement systems (principles 11–12), (iv) operational risk management (principle 17), and (v) tiered participation arrangements (principle 19).[15] As shown in Box 3, this paper has referenced only a subset of the key considerations believed to have a bearing on the Azerbaijani financial market infrastructure context.

### Box 3: Principles for Financial Market Infrastructures Key Considerations for Assessment of Clearing and Settlement in the Securities Market of Azerbaijan

- A financial market infrastructure (FMI) should provide incentives to participants and, where relevant, their customers to manage and contain the risks that they pose to the FMI (key consideration [KC]2. Pr. 3).
- A payment system or securities settlement system (SSS) should cover its current and, where they exist, potential future exposures to each participant fully with a high degree of confidence, using collateral and other equivalent financial resources (KC3. Pr. 4).
- An FMI should establish explicit rules and procedures that address fully any credit losses it may face as a result of any individual or combined default among its participants with respect to any of their obligations to the FMI (KC3. Pr. 4).
- An FMI should generally limit the assets it routinely accepts as collateral to those with low credit, liquidity, and market risks (KC1. Pr. 5).
- An FMI should establish prudent valuation practices and develop haircuts that are regularly tested and take into account stressed market conditions (KC1. Pr. 5).
- A payment system or SSS, including one employing a deferred net settlement mechanism, should maintain sufficient liquid resources in all relevant currencies to effect same-day settlement and, where appropriate, intraday or multiday settlement of payment obligations (KC3. Pr. 7).
- An FMI with access to central bank accounts, payment services, or securities services should use these services, where practical, to enhance its management of liquidity risk (KC8. Pr. 7).
- If an FMI allocates potentially uncovered liquidity shortfalls to its participants, the FMI should have clear and transparent rules and procedures for the allocation of shortfalls. These procedures could involve a funding arrangement between the FMI and its participants, the mutualization of shortfalls among participants according to a clear and transparent formula, or the use of liquidity rationing (3.7.19, Pr. 7).
- An FMI should complete final settlement by no later than the end of the value date, and preferably intraday or in real time, to reduce settlement risk (KC2. Pr. 8).
- An FMI should conduct its money settlements in central bank money, where practical and available, to avoid credit and liquidity risks (KC1. Pr. 9).

*continued on next page*

14 If the NDC does not play the role of CCP, 21 principles out of 24 can be applied, but if the NDC performs the role of CCP in addition to its current central securities depository/securities settlement system role, all 24 principles can be applied.

15 Credit risk (principle [Pr]. 4), collateral (Pr. 5), margin (Pr. 6), liquidity risk (Pr. 7), settlement finality (Pr. 8), money settlements (Pr. 9), Central Securities Depository (Pr. 11), exchange-of-value settlement systems (Pr. 12), and tiered participation arrangements (Pr. 19).

Box 3 *continued*

- If an FMI conducts money settlements on its own books, it should minimize and strictly control its credit and liquidity risks (KC4. Pr. 9).
- A move to a shorter cycle could generate increased settlement fails, with a higher proportion of participants unable to exchange settlement data or to acquire the necessary resources for settlement in the time available. Replacement cost risk would not be reduced as much as anticipated, and operational risk and liquidity risk could increase. (3.15, Recommendations for Securities Settlement Systems market-wide recommendations).
- Tiered participation arrangements typically create credit and liquidity exposures between direct and indirect participants. The management of these exposures is the responsibility of the participants and, where appropriate, subject to supervision by their regulators (Explanatory Note 3.19.8, Pr. 19).

Source: CPMI-IOSCO. 2012. *Principles for Financial Market Infrastructures.*

This paper focuses on the main settlement risks the NDC might be exposed to if it carries out the role of settlement agent by simply operating the current guarantee mechanism run by the existing settlement agents. Although operational risk is also a key issue, given the information constraints, this report did not address that issue. The Asian Development Bank (ADB) has had access to public information (such as the relevant laws), as well as to some internal rules provided by the NDC. As of the end of 2025, with no concrete business model for implementing the new legal amendment, the assessment was conducted based on plausible assumptions about future models.

## As Is: Current Model

This section explains the workflow of the current model in Table 1. Under the NDC's current DVP scheme, cash clearing is carried out by the NDC.[16] Meanwhile, final settlement is done across the correspondent accounts at the CBA when cash balances are prepared by the settlement agents with which the investment companies maintain contractual relations.

An investment company is required by a settlement agent to provide guarantees up to its trading limit for the settlement to be subsequently carried out. The trading limit scheme is illustrated in Figure 1. The guarantees can be provided in the following pre-deposited assets: (i) funds transferred (prefunded cash), (ii) financial pledges,[17] (iii) bank guarantees, and (iv) insurance contracts. Figure 2 illustrates the current clearing and settlement flows in on-exchange securities transactions.

16 Under the NDC rules for implementation of the post-trade system and clearing activities, clearing is defined as the activity of data collection, verification, reconciliation, netting of positions, ranking of obligations, and compensation of claims for determining the mutual obligations of the participants in the clearing process.

17 The terminology of "financial pledges" is used by the NDC.

**Figure 1: Trading Limit**

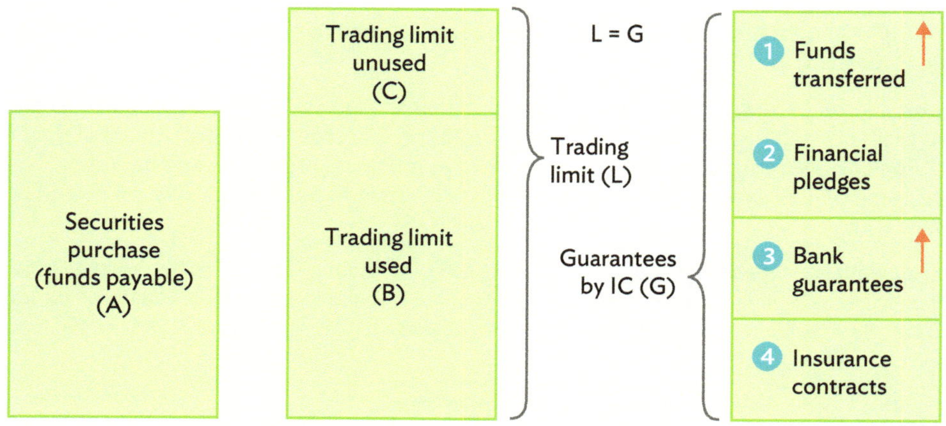


The trading limit (the "Limit" or "L") is the monetary amount set by the settlement agent (SA) to the investment company (IC) for the purchase of securities on the stock exchange during one trading day. The above figure is an illustration of the case of an IC transaction on day T. The limit (L) is set, with a buffer, as an amount larger than that of the securities purchased today (A). The limit is backed by the equivalent amount of guarantees (G), consisting of four pre-deposited items: (i) funds transferred (or prefunded cash), (ii) financial pledges, (iii) bank guarantees, and (iv) insurance contracts.

Trade limit setting considers only the funds being paid but does not take into account the funds being received. The limit can be set for the current day, or for a certain future period in advance. The limit can be updated daily. Funds and financial pledges should be deposited promptly to increase the limit. Thus, the current way of operating the limit is likely to function as an arrangement constraining transactions.

Source: Author.

There are three steps in the clearing and settlement process, as shown in Figure 2, for the case where the buy and sell-side investment companies are different.[18] First, in ① through ⑪, the investment company and the settlement agent agree on the trading limit amount, as the investment company should provide guarantees to the settlement agent, taking into account the client's and the investment company's proprietary trades. The settlement agent then inputs the trading limit amount into the NDC's internal system.[19] The investment company can also monitor its trading limit amount in this system. Depending on the security type, transactions are settled by applying DVP1 or DVP2. Irrespective of the DVP type, the securities and trading limit amounts are blocked once the orders are placed. The cash leg is then settled, and the securities leg is also settled. Within the trading limits, the cash leg payment is guaranteed by the settlement agent. Second, in ⑫, once the settlement is completed across the settlement agent's correspondent accounts at the CBA, the settlement agent makes payment to the investment company on the settlement agent's book. Third, in ⑬, the investment company credits or debits the client's account on the investment company's books.

[18] This case involves what are called "non-cross" transactions, while cross transactions occur when the buy- and sell-side investment companies are the same.

[19] This refers to the Central Electronic Depository of the Republic of Azerbaijan.

**Figure 2: Clearing and Settlement Flows in On-Exchange Securities Transactions**

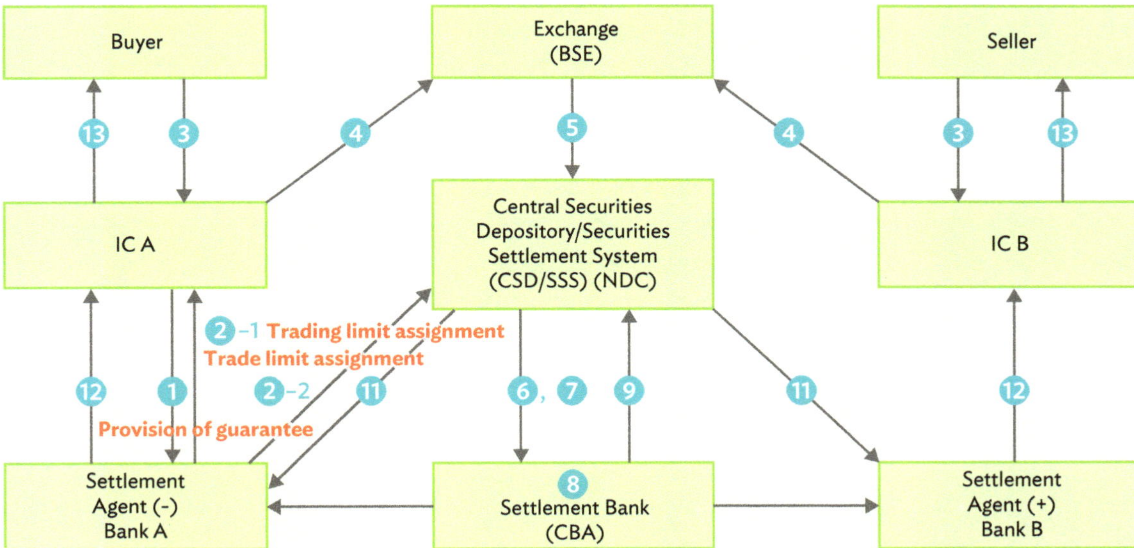


| Process | |
|---|---|
| 1 | Buyer-side investment company (IC) provides guarantees to the settlement agent (SA). |
| 2–1/2 | SA assigns a trading limit to the buyer-side IC and inputs it into the National Depository Center's (NDC) internal system. A trading limit can be set for the current day or for a certain future period in advance. |
| 3 | Investors (buyer and seller) give orders to IC. |
| 4 | ICs (buyer and seller sides) place orders on Baku Stock Exchange (BSE). |
| 5 | NDC system checks the securities balance of the seller-side IC and the trading limit of the buyer-side IC. If the balance and the trading limit are sufficient, the system blocks the relevant securities and the relevant part of the trading limit. |
| 6 | NDC carries out clearing. |
| 7 | NDC sends clearing results (liability report) to the Central Bank of the Republic of Azerbaijan (CBA) (T+0, T+1). |
| 8 | CBA carries out cash settlement between SAs (T+0, T+1). |
| 9 | CBA sends confirmation of cash settlement. |
| 10 | NDC carries out securities settlement (T+0, T+1). |
| 11 | NDC sends a report on transactions of IC to SA. |
| 12 | SA carries out cash settlement with IC (T+0, T+1). |
| 13 | IC carries out cash settlement with investors (T+0, T+1). |

Source: Drawn up by the technical assistance project based on NDC material.

## To Be (1): Baseline Model

Figure 3 illustrates the process reflecting the presumed role of the NDC under the baseline model per the amended law (para. 2), as the NDC has not disclosed the model it is considering. The difference between the current model and the baseline model is that the NDC now takes on the role of the settlement agent in the baseline model. The investment company will present the pledge agreements to the NDC, and the NDC (as pledgee) will carry out the pledge operation and assign the trading limit to the investment company (the pledger). The NDC thus assumes the roles of the existing eight settlement agents combined.[20] The NDC holds the cash accounts of participating institutions and operates an embedded funds transfer system, allowing for settlement of securities and funds within a single entity.

From a risk management perspective, steps ①–② and ⑦–⑧ highlighted in red are of interest in settlement risk management.

### Figure 3: Clearing and Settlement Flows Under NDC Model-to-Be

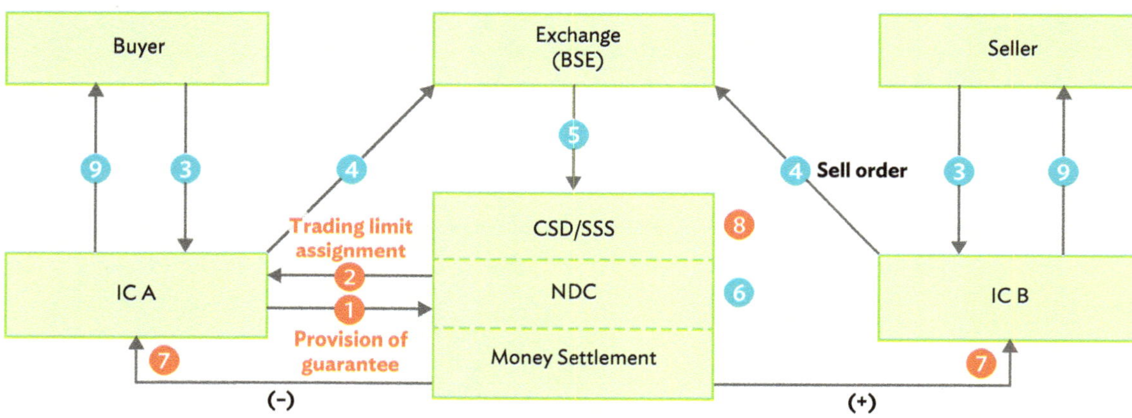


| | Process |
|---|---|
| 1 | Buyer-side investment company (IC) provides guarantees to the National Depository Center (NDC). |
| 2 | NDC assigns a trading limit to the buyer-side IC. A trading limit can be set for the current day or for a certain future period in advance. |
| 3 | Investors (buyer and seller) give orders to IC. |
| 4 | IC (buyer and seller sides) place orders on Baku Stock Exchange (BSE). |
| 5 | NDC system checks the securities balance of the seller-side IC and the trading limit of the buyer-side IC. If the trading limit and the balance are sufficient, the system blocks the relevant securities and the relevant part of the trading limit. BSE sends information to NDC. |
| 6 | NDC carries out clearing. |
| 7 | NDC carries out cash settlement between ICs if the paying IC has a sufficient amount in its accounts. |
| 8 | NDC carries out securities settlement. |
| 9 | IC carries out cash settlement with investors (T+0, T+1). |

CSD = Central Securities Depository, SSS = Securities Settlement System.
Source: Drawn up by the technical assistance project based on NDC material.

[20] The current *Joint Agreement on Clearing and Settlement of Securities and Derivatives* should be revised to designate the NDC as the settlement agent.

## To Be (2): Recommended Model

Figure 4 illustrates the process under the recommended model, where the NDC is designated as a CCP. The NDC performs the risk management roles in the cash market products, ensuring the settlement of securities and funds in transactions. The NDC assumes obligations in the clearing of securities transactions and undertakes netting to finalize the settlement details. Then it proceeds with the settlement process.

The NDC, acting as a CCP, performs various risk management tasks, including the assumption of obligations, netting, confirmation, and notification of settlement details, as well as managing risks through the implementation of margin, collateral, and default waterfall schemes. The NDC ensures stable settlement, serving as the entity responsible for the delivery of securities and transfer of funds. Risk is managed in a collaborative way among the clearing members.

As in the baseline model, the NDC holds the cash accounts of clearing members and operates an embedded funds transfer system, allowing for the settlement of securities and funds within the NDC. From a risk management perspective, steps ⑤–⑥ and ⑧–⑫ are of interest. In the future, issues may arise concerning the clearing of derivative products through the CCP.

## Comparison of Baseline and Recommended Models

For discussion purposes, comparisons among the current, baseline, and recommended models are presented in Table 2. The baseline model relies on the NDC to guarantee settlements, which could potentially lead to liquidity management constraints. The NDC might require cash prefunding, which could lead to trading restrictions. However, these drawbacks can be mitigated if liquidity from the central bank or a commercial bank is available. Not guaranteeing DVP1 transactions and allowing bilateral gross settlement via intraday repos/overdrafts are expected to significantly reduce the NDC's settlement guarantee burdens. For DVP2 transactions involving netting, under the baseline model, introducing a clearing fund and a margin arrangement can be used to manage settlement risks.

The recommended model proposes the establishment of a CCP to enhance transparency in settlement risk management and strengthen the crisis control capabilities. While there may be significant initial costs and operational challenges due to a lack of experience, the concentration of multiple functions within a single institution also requires careful consideration of operational risk management. If there are practical short-term constraints on CCP implementation, a phased approach could be considered, with the baseline model adopted initially and the transition to the recommended model undertaken later.

**Figure 4: Clearing and Settlement Flow Under Central Counterparty Model**

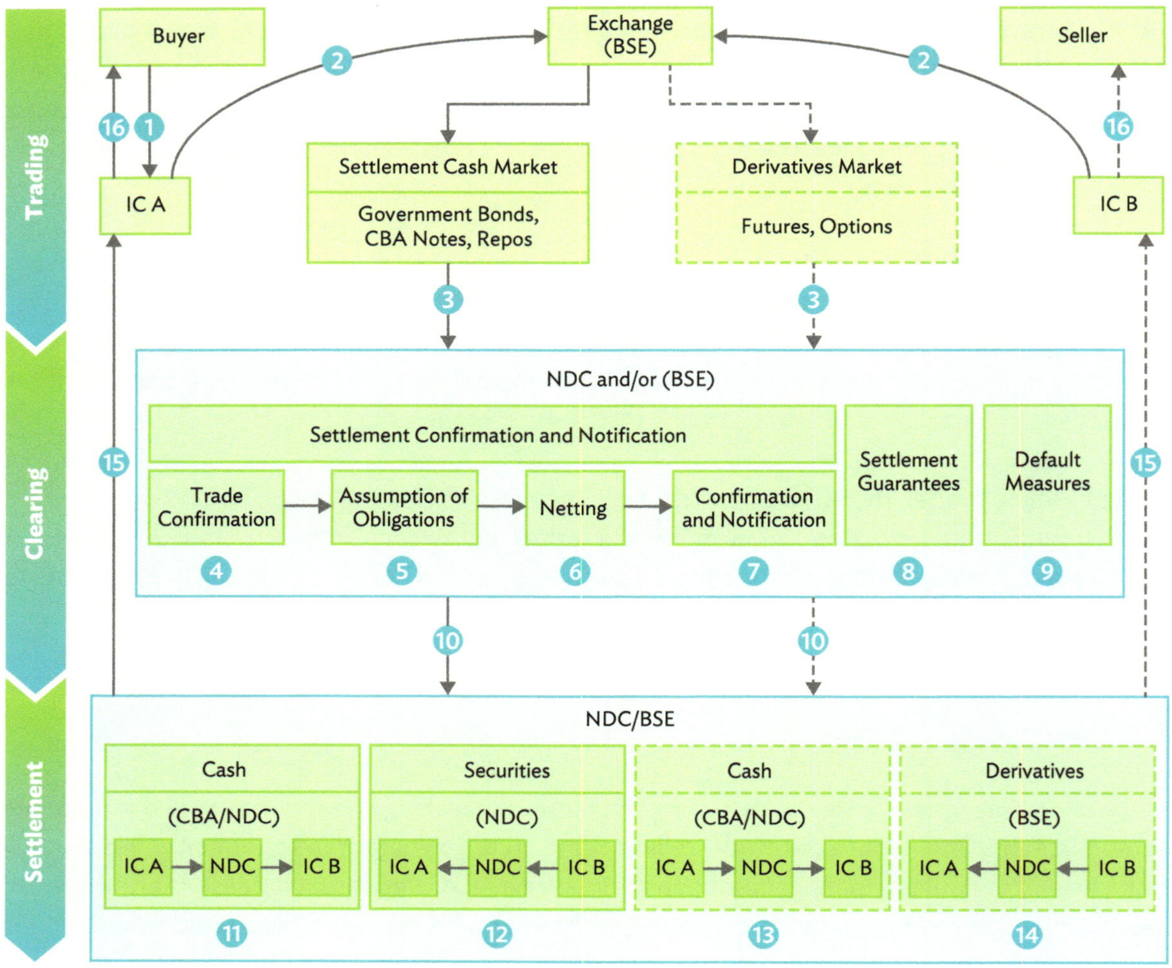


| | Process |
|---|---|
| 1 | Investors (buyer and seller) give orders to the investment company (IC). |
| 2 | ICs (buyer and seller sides) place orders on Baku Stock Exchange. |
| 3 | BSE sends information to the National Depository Center (NDC). |
| 4 | If the transaction details are corrected due to the occurrence of erroneous trading, NDC checks and reflects the corrections in the transaction confirmation. |
| 5 | Interposing itself between the seller and the buyer, NDC undertakes the assumption of liability and ensures the performance of the contract. |
| 6 | Overall settlement volume is significantly reduced through multilateral netting. The subjects of netting can be securities and funds. |
| 7 | NDC confirms the settlement details and notifies members of the transaction records. |
| 8, 9 | (Not applicable.) |
| 10 | NDC sends a settlement order. |

*continued on next page*

Figure 4 *continued*

| | Process |
|---|---|
| 11 | NDC checks the securities balance of the seller-side IC. If the balance is sufficient, the system blocks the relevant securities. NDC carries out cash settlement between ICs if a paying IC has a sufficient amount in its accounts. |
| 12 | NDC carries out securities settlement (for derivatives positions, netting is carried out). |
| 13, 14 | (Not applicable as of now.) |
| 15 | NDC carries out cash settlement with the investment company (T+0, T+1). |
| 16 | Investment company carries out cash settlement with investors (T+0, T+1). |

CBA = Central Bank of the Republic of Azerbaijan.
Note: Sequence numbers 13 and 14 are for derivative product clearings.
Source: Drawn up by the technical assistance project based on the contents of the flow chart in Korea Exchange. 2022. *Guide to Korea Exchange Clearing and Settlement*. Korea Exchange.

## Table 2: Comparison of Current and Potential Settlement Agent Models

| | Current Model | Baseline Model | Recommended Model |
|---|---|---|---|
| **Pros** | (i) Practical settlement guarantee services in absence of a CCP<br>(ii) Cost savings in IT infrastructure investment in low-volume trading environments<br>(iii) Mitigation of systemic risk is possible based on a prefunded scheme | (i) Reducing IT system investment cost while adapted within the current system<br>(ii) Improved transparency in risk management<br>(iii) Interim response in preparation for CCP establishment | (i) Response to increased transactions<br>(ii) Enhanced transparency in risk management<br>(iii) Long-term relief of clearing members' financial burdens<br>(iv) Improvement of FMI conditions for foreign investors<br>(v) Strengthened crisis addressing capabilities |
| **Cons** | (i) Possibility of trading constraints (increased management costs with a surge in transactions)<br>(ii) Settlement agent burdens for settlement risk management (collateral and intraday credit management)<br>(iii) Supervisory burdens on settlement agent (trading limit and fulfillment of settlement agent agreements)<br>(iv) Weak risk management by FMIs | (i) Absence of intraday credit provision by NDC, leading to liquidity risk exposure<br>(ii) Potential dependence on cash prefunding<br>(iii) New costs in establishing the liquidity facility by CBA<br>(iv) Possibility of increased complexity in risk management as NDC collaborates with existing settlement agents | (i) Initial costs incurred for legal and financial arrangements, IT system set-up, etc.<br>(ii) New costs in establishing the liquidity facility by CBA<br>(iii) Concentration risk (CSD/SSS/CCP/PS)<br>(iv) Increased operational risk management costs (backup systems) |

CBA = Central Bank of the Republic of Azerbaijan, CCP = central counterparty, CSD = central securities depository, FMI = financial market infrastructure, SSS = securities settlement system, PS = payment system.
Source: Author.

# 3 RISK ANALYSIS

## Baseline Model

Under the NDC's implementation of its new function, when money settlements are conducted on the NDC's books, the NDC should control credit and liquidity risks. Under the assumption that the current assignment of trading limits is undertaken by the NDC's settlement agent services, based on the guarantee mechanism only for DVP2 transactions and without the NDC's access to a central bank liquidity facility, liquidity and credit risk will be limited. It is assumed that DVP1 transactions are not guaranteed by the NDC. This assumption is for discussion purposes, utilizing the baseline model in Table 1. Evaluation of the baseline model reveals a potential risk implication in a situation where the NDC's liquidity management is insufficient.

## Credit and Liquidity Risk Management

The baseline model is assessed as follows, based on principles concerning (i) credit and liquidity risk, (ii) collateral, and (iii) other risk management issues. Risk factors may mutually affect each other because of the interactions among them.[21] Although this paper only considers selected issues, risk analysis should not necessarily be confined to the issues analyzed within this scope.

### *a. Credit Risk*

In the Azerbaijani securities market, settlement risks are managed by the trading limit setting to control credit and liquidity risks. In the baseline model, the NDC may require investment banks and investment companies to set pre-defined trading limits for the current day or for certain future periods in advance. Order amounts exceeding these trading limits are disallowed. Currently, when an investment company has exhausted its 100% trading limit, the investment company's buying order instructions are automatically suspended. The settlement agent is responsible for managing the trading limit by monitoring the unused portion throughout the day.

21 *PFMI*, p. 36.

If the NDC guarantees settlement, it must hold or borrow funds sufficient to settle DVP transactions. Requiring the investment company to fully prefund in cash, in advance, will also address the risk of settlement failure. In existing market practice (i.e., in the current model), it is likely for the settlement agent to extend intraday credit to the investment company to facilitate timely settlement. The potential risks to the existing settlement agent's exposure are referenced in Box 4. The NDC is not allowed to grant a credit extension to an investment company, however.

Therefore, to avoid risk, it is anticipated that the NDC will guarantee settlement through a mechanism fully prefunded by the investment companies. However, in this scenario, the NDC may allow transactions in a more restrictive manner than the existing settlement agents do.

To avoid this, the NDC can borrow funds from the money market to facilitate settlements within the pre-arranged trading limits. If the investment company goes bankrupt, the NDC should dispose of the noncash financial pledges that it received to cover the amount borrowed. However, if the NDC is forced to fire-sell the financial pledges (i.e., in extreme but plausible market conditions), it may not be able to repay the full amount borrowed and may therefore be exposed to credit risk.

In the baseline model, the NDC might not play a role in setting trading limits for DVP1 transactions, as it cannot guarantee them due to its limited liquidity management capacity. Ultimately, DVP1 does not entail credit risk, as settlement occurs when both the securities and the funds are ready, although this DVP1 mode still triggers replacement cost risk.[22]

### Box 4: Potential Credit and Liquidity Risks Borne by Settlement Agent

"Credit risk is broadly defined as the risk that a counterparty will be unable to fully meet its financial obligations when due or at any time in the future. The default of a participant (and its affiliates) can cause severe disruptions to financial market infrastructure, other participants, and the financial markets more broadly. Liquidity risk is the risk that a counterparty, whether a participant or another entity, will have insufficient funds to meet its financial obligations as and when expected, although it may be able to do so in the future."[a]

As the guarantee includes assets other than cash, an investment company may be short of cash at the time of settlement during a financial market crunch. In extreme circumstances, if the investment company goes into bankruptcy and does not eventually repay the intraday overdraft (if any) to the settlement agent, the settlement agent may face liquidity pressure first. Then, if the market disposal value of its collateral is less than the credit extended for the investment company, the settlement agent may also be exposed to credit risk. If the guarantee is fully prefunded in cash only, the settlement agent is not exposed to any risk. If the pre-deposited guarantee is sufficient, there will likely be no credit or liquidity risk.

a See the definitions of credit and liquidity risk in *Principles for Financial Market Infrastructures*, pp. 175, 177.
Source: Author.

22 The risk that a counterparty to an outstanding transaction of completion in the future will fail to perform on the settlement date. This failure may leave the solvent party with an unhedged or open market position or deny the solvent party unrealized gains or the position. See CPMI. 2016. *A Glossary of Terms Used in Payments and Settlement Systems.*

For DVP2 transactions, at present, funds are settled across the correspondent accounts at the CBA among the settlement agents, after multilateral netting by the NDC, at the designated time of 2:00 p.m. As the cash leg is settled in a netting mode, the DVP2 settlement model necessitates full cover to be compliant with the credit risk management requirement (see Box 3, KC3, Pr. 4). The current settlement agent's prearranged full cover guarantee approach is thus compliant with the PFMI credit risk requirement.

In a scenario where noncash pledges are allowed, if an investment company defaults, the NDC must procure funds to cover the payment obligation and subsequently liquidate the pledges to recover the funds. During this process, if their sale value is insufficient, the NDC may, in theory, be exposed to credit risk, although this scenario is unlikely. The main risk may stem from the composition of the guarantee mechanism's noncash items and the NDC's inability to obtain liquidity. If the pre-deposited guarantee is sufficient, the NDC will not be exposed to any credit risk. If the NDC sticks to a cash-only solution to ensure this, it might, however, constrain transactions. In view of this, alternative ways to alleviate the trading limit arrangement may be pursued to support transactions in the securities markets.

### *b. Liquidity Risk*

Under the baseline model, when the NDC performs multiple roles without having access to a liquidity facility, including the role of a CCP, the need for liquidity becomes larger. In accordance with the PFMI recommendations, the NDC may need to have sufficient liquid resources to effect same-day and intraday settlement of payment obligations under stress scenarios. It may have to prepare for the possible default of the participant and its affiliates, which would generate the largest aggregate payment obligation, known as the Cover 1 requirement.[23]

The NDC should prepare qualifying liquid resources, as recommended in Box 5, to meet liquidity needs for the Cover 1 requirement, since it is systemically important at the domestic level. It should perform stress tests, simulating the default of the participant, including its affiliates, with the largest payment obligation, as is recommended by the PFMI.

In the case of a participant default, in DVP2 settlements, financial pledges should be monetized on the same day through prearranged qualified liquid resources such as committed credit lines.

The NDC is not allowed to provide credit to participating institutions. In the event of a participant's default, the NDC cannot immediately dispose of the collateral and convert it into cash, so it must raise liquidity to complete daily settlement. In this case, it should secure committed credit lines with commercial banks, as recommended in Box 6, or it may have a way to raise liquidity from the central bank.

23 Cover 1 refers to the preparation of liquidity for the possible default of the participant and its affiliates with the largest payment obligation, while Cover 2 refers to the case of the default of two participants and their affiliates. Cover 2 is applied to financial market infrastructures that are globally systemically important.

**Box 5: Maintain Sufficient Liquid Resources for Payment Systems and Securities Settlement Systems**

A payment system or securities settlement system, including one employing a deferred net settlement[a] mechanism, should maintain sufficient liquid resources in all relevant currencies to effect same-day settlement, and where appropriate intraday or multiday settlement, of payment obligations with a high degree of confidence under a wide range of potential stress scenarios that should include, but not be limited to, the default of its affiliates that would generate the largest aggregate payment obligation in extreme but plausible market conditions.

a A net settlement mechanism which settles on a net basis at the end of a predefined settlement cycle.
Source: CPMI-IOSCO. *Principles for Financial Market Infrastructures,* Key Consideration 3, Principle 7.

**Box 6: Qualifying Liquid Resources**

For meeting its minimum liquid resource requirement, a financial market infrastructure's qualifying liquid resources in each currency include cash at the central bank of issue and at creditworthy commercial banks, committed lines of credit, committed foreign exchange swaps, and committed repos, as well as highly marketable collateral held in custody and investments that are readily available and convertible into cash with prearranged and highly reliable funding arrangements, even in extreme but plausible market conditions.

Source: CPMI-IOSCO. Principles for Financial Market Infrastructures. Key Consideration 5, Principle 7.

If an investment company or investment bank does not fulfill its payment obligations, "the NDC should immediately inform the CBA of this, and calculate fines imposed on the investment bank or investment company daily until its obligations are fulfilled. The NDC is not allowed to carry out any operations until its obligations are fulfilled."[24] If the default were not solved by the end of the value date, risks might spread. The NDC, in conducting settlement agent services, has limited capacity to address liquidity pressures in the event of severe market distress. Thus, measures to alleviate the NDC's liquidity constraints should be put in place.

### c. *Collateral*

"Collateral is defined as an asset or third-party commitment that a collateral provider uses to secure an obligation vis-à-vis a collateral taker."[25] In this section, collateral is assumed to refer to noncash assets, such as financial pledges, bank guarantees, and insurance contracts, included in the guarantee provided by the investment company to the settlement agent.

24 National Depository Center. 2019. *Rules of the Post-Trade System and Clearing Activities* (11. Failure to perform obligations).
25 *PFMI*, p. 175.

The above-detailed credit and liquidity risks are closely related to the collateral posted for the guarantees. The required guarantees for the trading limit set by the settlement agent include cash (prefunded), financial pledges, bank guarantees, and insurance contracts. At present, this publication does not try to assess the quality and market values of the guarantees held by the settlement agents.

The *PFMI* states that guarantees are not acceptable as collateral, but adds the caveat that "in rare circumstances, and subject to regulatory approval, a guarantee fully backed by collateral that is realizable on a same-day basis may serve as acceptable collateral."[26]

It is also expected that specific wrong-way risk be prevented, with a financial market infrastructure required "to prohibit members from depositing securities issued by themselves, and to prohibit further the use of securities issued by the affiliates of clearing members as collateral."[27] "The financial market infrastructure should also avoid concentrated holdings of certain assets."[28] Table 3 details the eligible collateral and pledges accepted by select institutions.

The NDC is expected to follow the general requirements that a financial market infrastructure should limit the assets that it accepts as collateral to those having low credit, liquidity, and market risks. In the event of a participant's bankruptcy, the NDC may be required to sell the collateral to recover the necessary funds. If the NDC were to guarantee settlement, it might be exposed

## Table 3: Eligible Collateral

| National Depository Center[a] | Euroclear[b] | Korea Exchange[c] | Japan Securities Clearing Corporation[d] |
|---|---|---|---|
| Cash | Proprietary collateral | Eligible | Cash (JPY, USD) |
| Financial pledges | Cash deposits | Cash | Japanese government bonds |
| Bank guarantees<br>Insurance contracts | Related/unrelated party arrangements | Foreign currencies<br>Government bonds | Bonds guaranteed by the government. |
| | Customer asset pledges (subject to consent), etc. | Central bank bonds | Foreign government bonds |
| | | Special bonds, etc. | Stocks |
| | | Eligibility assessment | Municipal bonds |
| | | Listed stocks | Special bonds |
| | | Corporate bonds | Corporate bonds, etc. |

JPY = Japanese yen, USD = US dollar

a Central Bank of the Republic of Azerbaijan. 2023. Joint Agreement on Clearing and Settlement of Securities and Derivatives.

b In the event of a participant default, Euroclear Bank has the right to immediately appropriate pledges of securities. Euroclear Bank and CPMI-IOSCO. 2023. Euroclear Bank–CPMI-IOSCO Disclosure Framework 2022, p. 63.

c CPMI-IOSCO. 2022. Principles for Financial Market Infrastructures: Disclosure Framework and Assessment Methodology, p. 62.

d Japan Securities Clearing Corporation has a fundamental policy of only accepting collateral with low credit, liquidity, and market risk. Footnote c, p. 51.

Source: Author.

26 *PFMI,* footnote 63, p. 46.

27 *PFMI*, Explanatory Note 3.5.3., p. 47.

28 *PFMI*, p. 48

to risk if the securities sold in a fire sale are worth less than the funds required. When there is a need to urgently adjust the trading limit to respond to rapidly growing transactions, appropriate arrangements to secure additional funds should be in place. In this light, it would be desirable to define and include the committed credit line as an explicit item among the types of guarantees.

Depending upon their agreement, a client can allow its securities to be used by an investment company for the investment company's financial pledges to meet the trading limit. However, if the investment company goes into bankruptcy without returning its clients' assets, the client's assets can be exposed to credit risk. The NDC should protect clients' assets by prohibiting an investment company from commingling its clients' assets with its own assets to satisfy the trading limit.

### *d. Other Risk Issues*

In the baseline model, the NDC can act as the settlement institution for investment companies. As settlement takes place on the books of the NDC, the settlement asset used is a claim on the NDC. "The credit and liquidity risks associated with a claim on the [NDC] are therefore directly related to the [NDC]'s overall credit and liquidity risks."[29] Thus, ensuring the NDC's sound management is a key issue. In this light, "general business risk refers to the potential losses arising from the [NDC]'s operations as a business enterprise that are not related to a participant default."[30] If there is an impairment of the NDC's financial position, the going concern issue might arise. To address this risk, the NDC might be required "to hold liquid net assets funded by equity equal to at least [6] months of current operating expenses."[31]

When the NDC provides cash settlement services on its own books, one concern is liquidity fragmentation among participants, as they deposit their funds on the NDC's books. It should be determined whether the NDC should also have a way of using central bank money in realizing settlements, as is recommended in Box 7. One way would be to link the accounts of the CBA and the NDC. If the NDC is connected to the CBA's account, it can enjoy a number of benefits such as real-time gross settlement services, settlement in central bank money, and the availability of other useful central banking services.

**Box 7: Money Settlement**

A financial market infrastructure should conduct its money settlements in central bank money where it is practical and available. If central bank money is not used, a financial market infrastructure should minimize and strictly control the credit and liquidity risk arising from its use of commercial bank money.

Source: CPMI-IOSCO. Principles for Financial Market Infrastructures, Key Consideration 1, Principle 9.

29 *PFMI*, KC 3.9.7.
30 *PFMI*, Principle 15.
31 *PFMI*, Principle 15, Explanatory Note 3.15.5. The requirement for liquid net assets is equity rather than long-term liabilities.

The NDC is likely to be a highly integrated system that includes the operations of a central securities depository (CSD) and a securities settlement system (SSS). The payment system will be embedded in the SSS when the NDC provides cash account services for participants. The NDC might potentially become a CCP in the future, too. With this concentration of functions within a single entity, a potential operational risk concern—the single point of failure problem—could arise. The NDC's business continuity would be key to the stability of Azerbaijan's financial market. The recovery time and a backup facility should be addressed, but this report does not cover them.

## Recommended Model

Azerbaijan does not currently have a CCP, and risk analysis is constrained because it has not been determined which securities a CCP would clear. Based on the model set earlier, this section will focus on risks that may arise in CCP clearing processes for shares and government bonds, referencing cases that emerged during the 2008 global financial crisis. The discussion will be limited to credit and liquidity risks. The potential risks the CCP could face from an investment company's bankruptcy are examined. These cases are considered applicable to all CCPs.

"CCPs have the potential to reduce risks to market participants significantly through multilateral netting of trades and by imposing more effective risk controls on all participants."[32] However, introducing a CCP does not eliminate risks entirely. Since the risks incurred by clearing members can be transferred to the CCP, the PFMI strongly recommends that CCPs meet risk management requirements, stating that "the effectiveness of a CCP's risk control and the adequacy of its financial resources are critical to achieving these risk reduction benefits."

### Credit and Liquidity Risk

In the CCP, risks manifest in a concentrated form. Figure 5 examines the types of risks the NDC may face as the CCP for share and government bond transactions, specifically in the event of an investment company's insolvency. The credit and liquidity risks may arise together.

#### *a. Shares*

If investment company A defaults on its obligations, the NDC, following the procedures specified in its operational rules, halts the settlement for share transactions at that point and subsequently suspends the assumption of further obligations. When the transactions are halted, the NDC executes the close-out liquidation.[33] If insufficient funds are available due to investment company A's payment default on the bankruptcy date, the NDC needs to secure the necessary funds from the market or a cash collateral pool, which is an item of the default fund.

32 *PFMI*, p. 9.

33 This is the process undertaken by the CCP to liquidate or handle a defaulting participant's positions or obligations. It may involve selling the underlying assets or offsetting positions with other clearing members.

The NDC must have sufficient qualified liquid resources, including settlement reserves, a default fund, and credit lines, to inject funds immediately in cases of liquidity shortages. As shown in Figure 5, in the event of the bankruptcy of investment company A, the NDC first faces liquidity pressure to cover payment obligations. To prepare for this, adequate liquidity should be prearranged, and provisions such as an initial margin and a default fund should be appropriately established to facilitate timely payments. While this example illustrates the use of liquidity borrowed from the market, the utilization of a prearranged, committed credit line to obtain liquidity from multiple sources would be desirable. If a forced sale occurs during the liquidation process and a loss exceeds the amount originally raised, this can pose a risk to the NDC.

Therefore, the NDC needs to manage and mitigate credit risk by monitoring current exposures and potential future exposures. To achieve this, the NDC should calculate and impose appropriate margins and monitor the financial conditions of its members.

To prepare for the risk of a participant default, financial resources such as settlement reserves and funds contributed mutually by participants should be prearranged. Utilization of financial resources in stress situations should be simulated, and contingency plans should be in place for losses exceeding the prearranged resources. Procedures for using settlement resources to cover losses when a participant defaults should be well prepared.

**Figure 5: Credit Risk and Liquidity Risk Scenario for Share**

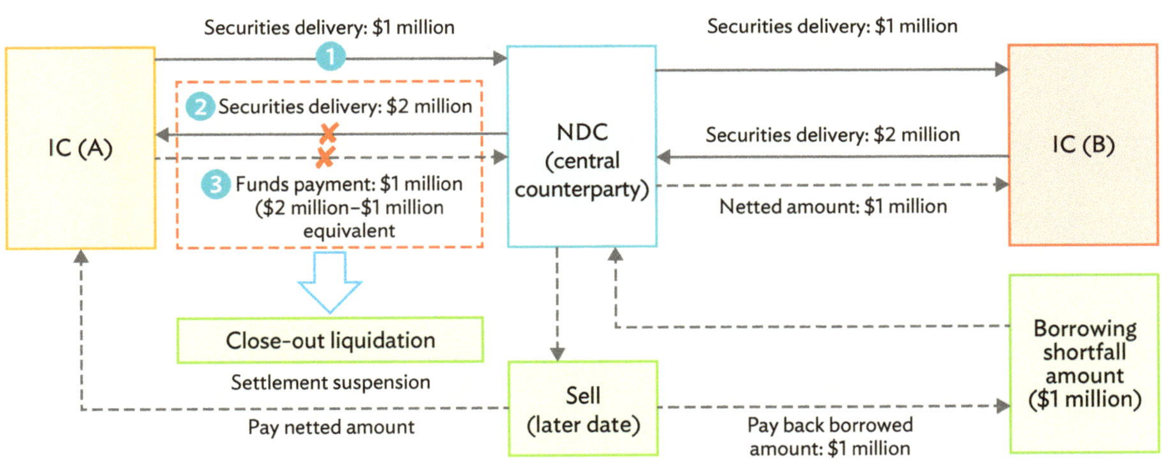


Note: Let us take as an example the crisis scenario shown here, where an investment company (IC) (A) with transactions outstanding has gone bankrupt. At the point of the bankruptcy of IC (A), and as a counterparty in the transactions, the National Depository Center (NDC) has already assumed the obligations of ICs. As a result, there are claims and obligations between the bankrupt IC (A) and solvent IC (B), involving (1) a share delivery (IC (A) to NDC), (2) a second share delivery (NDC to IC (A)), and (3) a fund payment (IC (A) to NDC, representing the netted amount between (1) and (2)). Notably, (1) involves the delivery of shares from the bankrupt IC (A) to the NDC before the NDC decides to suspend the assumption of obligations. In this scenario, a close-out liquidation is conducted, specifically for (2) and (3), as seen within the red dotted lines. For (1), the NDC receives the shares from the bankrupt IC (A) before deciding to suspend assumption of obligations. Consequently, owing to (3), there is a shortfall in the funds that were expected to be received from the bankrupt IC (A). To address the funding shortfall, the NDC borrows funds from the money market or utilizes a cash collateral pool. In this example, the NDC disposes of the shares, using the proceeds from the sale to pay back the borrowed funds from the market.
Source: Modified by technical assistance project based on the contents of Bank of Japan Research Paper. 2009. *The Bankruptcy of Lehman Brothers and Its Impact on the Japanese Payment System.*

### *b. Government Bonds*

In a scenario where government bonds are CCP-cleared through the NDC and an investment company undergoes bankruptcy, a close-out liquidation is executed. Subsequently, operations are conducted with the affected investment company for the following purposes:

(i) *To secure the necessary funds for receiving government bonds scheduled for delivery from the seller*, the approach involves the utilization of a committed credit line and fund acquisition through repo transactions. When the committed credit line is insufficient, ad hoc repo or other transactions can be arranged to secure additional funds.

(ii) *To procure the government bonds from the bankrupt investment company and deliver them to the buying member*. Failures to deliver securities (fails) can accumulate daily until the government bonds are acquired from the bankrupt investment company. These fails may escalate and contribute to larger fails in other bond transactions. After the government bonds are procured, fails can decrease.

This operational approach emphasizes the utilization of committed credit lines and repo transactions and the effective solution of fail risks to ensure the smooth functioning of the market under challenging circumstances.

# 4 ROAD MAP FOR NATIONAL DEPOSITORY CENTER SETTLEMENT AGENT SERVICE

## Near-Term: Baseline Model

The amended law permits the NDC to provide cash accounts to designated financial entities.[34] Based on the gap analysis of the NDC-guaranteed scheme, directions for improvement are derived to design NDC settlement services consistent with international standards and practices. Considering the NDC's significant roles in Azerbaijani securities clearing and settlement, a holistic approach was taken in exploring extensive measures for improvement. Table 4 presents transition options.

As an interim transition, per the baseline model, the current guarantee mechanism will be applied to only DVP2 transactions that require full-cover responsibility. However, the NDC may also be exposed to liquidity risks when managing DVP2 if it lacks sufficient liquidity. To avoid such risks, the current guarantee mechanism backed by financial pledges should be maintained, and, in preparation against a participant's default, a procedure for obtaining liquidity from the liquidity provider, by pledging collateral, should be arranged.[35] Furthermore, a loss-sharing fund could be established to address the possibility that financial pledges fall short of the resources needed in extreme market conditions.[36] A scheme is sought under which DVP1 transactions will not be guaranteed, subject to the central bank's liquidity provision.

The current settlement agent-guaranteed scheme needs to eventually move to a CCP-guaranteed one. Under the recommended model, settlement will be ensured by a CCP risk management framework that includes margins, a default fund, and the use of a sequence of prefunded financial resources (waterfall).

With this transition in mind, preliminary directions toward it might include (i) a robust implementation plan for settlement agent service provision by the NDC, (ii) a plan for central bank service provision, and (iii) a review of the existing trading limit-based guarantee mechanism. Further detailed checks and reviews of these issues, through knowledge-sharing events or consultations, will be conducted in the coming months to address the Azerbaijani context.

34 At an internal discussion on this paper among selected staff from the Bank of Korea and the Korea Exchange, there were two differing opinions: one suggesting that the NDC should directly adopt the CCP model, and the other advocating for the baseline model.

35 Considering the asset classes processed in DVP2 transactions (mainly corporate bonds and shares), the liquidity provider might be the commercial banks, through prearranged committed credit lines, unlike in the case of DVP1 for government bonds and central bank notes.

36 In Chapter 6 of the law, the establishment of a clearing fund is articulated in Articles 50 and 58.

**Table 4: Transition Options**

| | Current Model (Fully Guaranteed) | Baseline Model (Partially Guaranteed)[a] | Recommended Model (CCP-Guaranteed) |
|---|---|---|---|
| Settlement guarantee | Yes (DVP1) | No (DVP1) | No (DVP1) |
| | Yes (DVP2) | Yes (DVP2) | Yes (DVP2) |
| CCP function | No | No | Yes |

CCP = central counterparty, DVP = delivery versus payment, DVP1 = securities and funds settled on a gross basis, DVP2 = securities settled on a gross and funds on a net basis.
Note: The fully guaranteed and partially guaranteed classifications depend on whether DVP1 transactions are guaranteed.
Source: Author.

## Robust Plan for Settlement Agent Service Provision by the National Depository Center

In Azerbaijan, the CBA recognizes the need for fostering the capital market, and in line with this, the Law was amended in 2023. This amendment is likely to heighten competition among the banking industry and investment companies. The CBA has tried to ensure a state of equality. In this vein, in accordance with the law, the NDC can open cash accounts for participating financial institutions, leading to settlements of both securities and funds within a single entity. The main issue is how the NDC will manage the clearing and settlement risks under the new scheme.

The NDC plans to carry out its new function of cash settlement, adding to its existing function of securities settlement. The NDC may intend to offer cash accounts to its participants by providing them with direct claims on the NDC itself. However, the NDC is much less likely to be able to manage liquidity risk than large, deposit-taking commercial banks.

A robust plan for NDC implementation of its settlement agent services, including a set of risk management tools, should be prepared. Currently, the NDC is preparing to address its role as a settlement agent service provider. In devising the NDC's arrangements, the following issues could be considered.

First, the NDC should avoid exposure to credit and liquidity risks when it operates the current settlement guarantee mechanism and performs the role previously undertaken by the settlement agents. As has been explained, in the event of an investment company's bankruptcy, the NDC may also be exposed to risks.

The NDC should prepare an arrangement for "completing final settlement by no later than the end of the value date, and preferably intraday or in real time, to reduce settlement risks."[37] For default management, a clearly defined procedure should be in place. If a participant (investment company or investment bank) defaults, failing to make a cash payment by the specified time of settlement

37 *PFMI*, KC2, Principle 8.

in DVP2, the NDC may need a prearranged committed credit line from commercial banks against financial pledges.[38] To this end, the NDC should have entered into prior agreements with the commercial banks.

In the event of a participant's insolvency, the NDC should dispose of the financial pledges provided by that participant. The procedures necessary for the sale of collateralized assets should be prepared after a detailed review. A typical example of net settlement risk management in the payment system is shown in Box 8.

The NDC's cash account structure should be determined in light of its practical use of central bank and commercial bank money. Under such an arrangement, a financial market infrastructure can back up settlements conducted on its own books with balances held in its central bank accounts.[39] Incorporating this arrangement, a way of supporting the NDC's cash settlement with central bank money could be devised. In this setting, preventing liquidity fragmentation might be considered. Linking the CBA and NDC accounts will facilitate the NDC's access to central banking services.[40]

A conceptual model applying the account linkages of the payment systems in Sweden or the United Kingdom could be referenced.[41] These are examples of the setting up of accounts, such as mirroring accounts and omnibus accounts,[42] which are offered to regulated payment system

### Box 8: Net Settlement Risk Management in DVP2 Cash-Leg (Example)

**Use of committed credit lines and disposal of collateral.** If any participant fails to meet its obligations for net settlement of transactions for which it provides collateral, the governor of the central bank may dispose of or use them as collateral against the commercial banks' credit lines. The disposal of collateralized securities shall be executed at the market price, and its method, timing, etc. shall be decided too.

**Loss sharing.** If, although the above measures have been taken, a shortage of settlement funds is not covered, all other net settlement participants shall share in making up the shortfall. An individual net settlement participant's share in making up a shortage of settlement funds shall be calculated in proportion to the amount of its collateralized securities to be provided or the amount of transactions to meet obligations arising from transactions for which net settlement is executed.

Notwithstanding the above provision, in the event of subsequent failure by any participant to share in making up the shortfall, the uncovered amount shall be again shared among the remaining participants in the relevant proportions.

Source: Technical assistance project-modified discussion version based on Bank of Korea. 2003. *Regulation on the Operation and Management of the Payment and Settlement Systems.*

38 The NDC may establish prearranged agreements with broker and/or dealers to sell collateral in an anonymized manner, adhering to confidentiality agreements.

39 *PFMI*, 3.9.7.

40 Recent cases of account linkages between central banks and payment system operators might be leveraged to get some idea of this approach.

41 See Central Bank of Sweden (Riksbank). 2023. *Rix-RTGS Instructions.* ("The sum of funds in all settlement accounts at the BiR [payments in real time] is always equal to, and backed by, the funds in central bank money in the Bankgirot's fiduciary account, which eliminates credit risk.").

42 Bank of England. 2021. *Omnibus Accounts—Access Policy.*

operators[43] to back up external payment systems or pool participant funds. These models enable the payment systems to back up their settlements in central bank money. The advantage of such a scheme is that it ensures participants' funds are protected and that counterparty credit risk in external payment systems is closely monitored and controlled.

Along the same lines, a policy for providing access to a central bank account should be reviewed by the CBA. If such access is allowed, the number of communications and messages may increase, as the two books of the central bank and the NDC are linked. Considering the computer capacities currently available, however, this would pose no serious barrier to system implementation.

In addition to the account linkage between the CBA and the NDC, a network to link the investment companies and investors in the steps of pre-trade and post-trade business processes needs to be arranged. These rules and frameworks need to be designed with investor protection against fraud and cybercrime in mind. In particular, stable payment services for securities transactions ensure safety and efficiency in the investment activities of securities market participants, and thereby directly support development of the securities market. The meticulous design and operation of payment services are thus essential.

## Central Bank's Intraday Liquidity Provision

To achieve safe and efficient securities settlement, liquidity provision by the central bank may help address settlement delays and the potential risks to the settlement agent.

The central bank might examine options for providing intraday liquidity to the NDC and investment banks to support settlement of government bonds in the exchange-traded and over-the-counter markets. It might also encourage financial institutions to settle their transactions processed through the Azerbaijan Interbank Payment System earlier during the day. Depending on the credit extension policy scheme, the central bank might consider the possibility of providing the settlement liquidity in the form of intraday repos or intraday overdrafts. Financial companies whose volumes of settlement remain negligible would be excluded from this intraday liquidity program. To prevent financial companies from becoming excessively reliant on the central bank, liquidity could be provided only for purchases of certain eligible securities, including government bonds, government-guaranteed bonds, and central bank notes.

Meanwhile, to avoid any impact on day-to-day monetary policy, an arrangement should be set up for the collection of all intraday liquidity supplied by the CBA by the end of the day of its issuance. Options possible include (i) a nonbank financial institution receives intraday liquidity from the central bank through the commercial banks, or (ii) a nonbank financial institution receives liquidity directly from the central bank, as seen in the case of the institution receiving repos (Figure 6). The Bank of Korea adopts the latter option. The Bank of Japan also implements a simultaneous processing of DVP and collateralization functions (Figure 7) providing intraday overdrafts.

43 When the NDC runs cash accounts on its books, the NDC operates the payment system in practice.

**Figure 6: Scheme for Daylight Liquidity Supply for Securities Settlement (Example)**

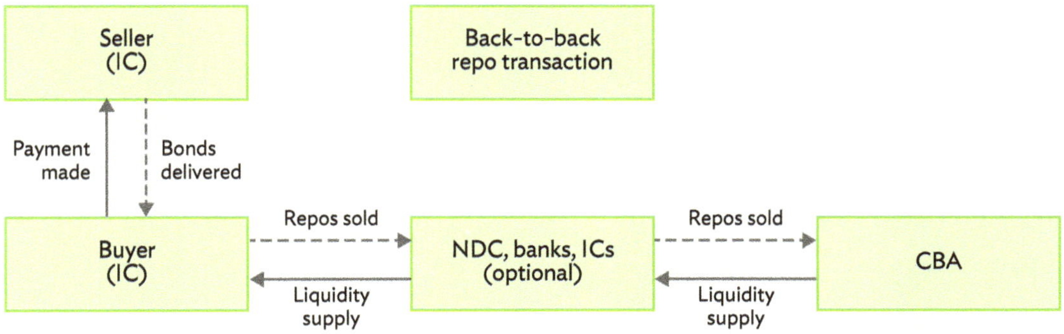


CBA = Central Bank of the Republic of Azerbaijan, IC = investment company, NDC = National Depository Center.
Source: Asian Development Bank consultants (based on the Bank of Korea intraday repo framework).

**Figure 7: Simultaneous Processing of Delivery Versus Payment and Collateralization Function**

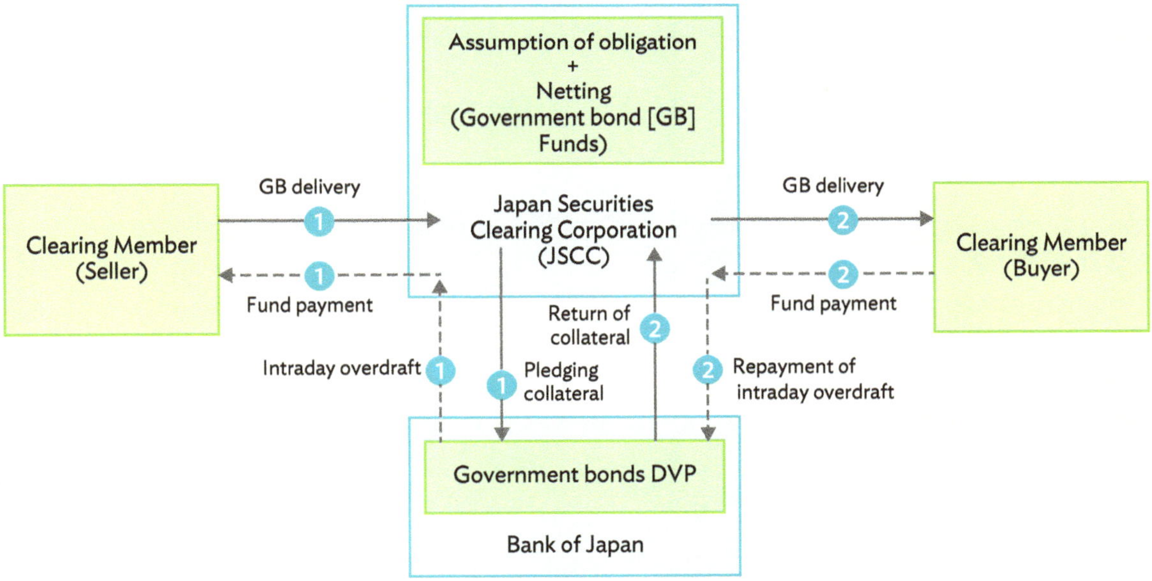


Note: The Bank of Japan calls this the simultaneous processing of delivery versus payment [DVP] and collateralization(SPDC) function. The SPDC function enables financial institutions that purchase Japanese government securities (JGSs) to receive intraday overdrafts from the Bank by using the JGSs that the institutions receive from the sellers as collateral, and then to use the funds to pay for such JGSs. This function is used to reduce the volume of liquidity necessary for settlement and to conduct smooth JGS settlement on a DVP basis. The JSCC makes use of the self-collateralization mechanism for its DVP settlement.
Source: Bank of Japan. 2004. *Functions and Operations of the Bank of Japan*. Chapter IV: Payment and Settlement and the Roles of the Bank of Japan.

The final decision depends upon the CBA's credit extension policy, given the relevant legal framework. The CBA should also undertake its own real-time monitoring of fund flows arising from this credit provision.

## Reviewing Counterparty Default Management Based on the Guarantee Scheme

In Azerbaijan, securities are settled based on a guarantee mechanism. Risks in the securities market are managed so that an individual settlement agent controls them by imposing a trading limit on an investment company's securities trades.

This practice appears to be aimed at providing market participants with some protection against losses from counterparty defaults. In the Azerbaijani market, "where a CCP does not exist, the guarantee mechanism has provided market participants with practical ways of protection against counterparty credit risks" over the last decades.[44]

Settlements of securities transactions are guaranteed by trading limits backed by prefunded cash as well as financial pledges, bank guarantees, and insurance contracts. These are prepared at the initial trading stage, and buy-side orders are executed by blocking the securities based on the corresponding trading limit. The settlement agent guarantees settlements of DVP1 transactions, subject to the trading limit. DVP1 does not, in fact, invite credit risk, although it may still trigger replacement cost risk. This approach to risk management might lead to fewer incentives for participants to engage in efficient risk management. [45]

Notwithstanding its positive effects on risk control, the current imposition of trading limits has the potential to adversely affect securities transactions. The trading limit is dependent on the individual settlement agent's capacity to guarantee settlement. Thus, if the transaction demand grows larger, the current trading limit arrangement might constrain transactions. In major securities markets around the world, a way of avoiding the unlimited expansion of payments may be applied on the securities buy side in ways such as setting a net debit cap to ensure that the buy side settles within the trading limit.[46] However, the restrictive trading limit arrangement (see Figure 1), coupled with the guarantee scheme, has been cited as a barrier to more active trading in the securities market.

Meanwhile, the settlement scheme in the primary market might be reviewed along with the review of the guarantee mechanism for DVP1 transactions (Box 9).

44 In markets where a CCP does not exist, a guarantee arrangement may provide market participants with some degree of protection against losses from counterparty defaults. See *PFMI*, footnote 11, p. 9.

45 Payment is guaranteed under a central planning system, and counterparties in transactions have no need to be concerned about payment system risks. Summers, B. 1994. *The Payment System, Design, Management, and Supervision*. International Monetary Fund.

46 In Japanese stock settlement, if buying is greater than selling, the member company transfers the covered funds to the CCP through its trading financial institution to manage risk. For the United States Depository Trust Company, participating institutions manage risk by counting their securities now held, the amounts paid, and the securities received. The collateral status of participants is monitored in the collateral management system in real time.

### Box 9: Risk Management for Government Bond Settlement in the Korean Primary Market

The Bank of Korea (BOK), acting as the government bond issuing agent, does not bear credit risk in the government bond issuance process. Following the completion of financial transactions with participating institutions, the BOK records changes in the register. If payment is not received within the designated period, the corresponding bid or allocation is considered void. The same principle applies to the issuance of Monetary Stabilization Bonds by the BOK, where failure to make payment within the specified time results in the invalidation of the allocation or bid.

The BOK does not undertake any obligation to guarantee payment to participating institutions. In the case of temporarily insufficient account balances, participating institutions (such as primary dealers or the government) manage liquidity risk through the BOK's intraday overdrafts and intraday repos.

Source: Bank of Korea. 2021. *Explanation of Securities Business by the Bank of Korea.*

Subject to the CBA's liquidity provision being ensured, it is recommended that there be a move away from the current settlement practices in DVP1 transactions, which rely on "trading limits and guarantees," to a system in which DVP 1 transactions are supported with "margin management," if necessary. A transition to standard DVP1 settlement is necessary. For DVP1 transactions in which a transaction between the two parties is settled by them on their own, the method of guaranteeing settlement and imposing a trading limit for this purpose deviates from the common practice in most markets in the world.

Notably, when DVP1 transactions for government bonds are mainly among brokers and/or dealers, a guarantee is less necessary. The current guarantee mechanism for DVP1 transactions could thus be dropped in favor of risk management, depending upon the credit bases of the transacting parties. Securities transactions between two parties need to move toward a way in which both parties manage the risks. If necessary, imposing a margin (good faith deposit) could be considered. As shown in Box 10, the margin can be set based on the replacement cost estimated from changes in government bond prices over a given period.[47]

In Azerbaijan, the settlement cycle is short compared to those in major jurisdictions. Generally, preparing funds for settlement within a short time frame is considered burdensome for financial companies, even though such a short time frame can reduce exposure among participants. When the CCP clearing function is introduced, use of a T+1 settlement cycle (instead of T+0) may also be reviewed, as well as overhauling the trading practices by, for example, allowing a securities fail arrangement.[48] This issue can also be reviewed in terms of the access of foreign investors to the Azerbaijani market. Nevertheless, the settlement cycle issue is subject to debate among market practitioners, and some products may justify the use of a T+0 cycle.

47 In the Republic of Korea market, the yield change during 1 business day has reached a historic maximum level of less than 3%.

48 A security fail is a transaction in which the securities and cash are not exchanged as agreed on the settlement date, usually because of technical and temporary causes.

## Box 10: Margin for Securities Market
### (Examples in the Republic of Korea and Japan)

Assuming the National Depository Center does not perform the role of central counterparty (CCP), the variation margin is not considered here, but only the initial margin is used to address the replacement cost risk in on-exchange delivery-versus-payment (DVP)1 transactions in Azerbaijan. The "initial margin is the collateral that is collected to cover potential changes in the value of each participant's position (that is, potential future exposure) over the appropriate close-out period in the event that the participant defaults."[a] Margin setting can be studied for its introduction in Azerbaijan, referencing the cases of on-exchange and over-the-counter (OTC) markets. The Korea Exchange, which is also a CCP in the Republic of Korea, applies a member margin only for stocks, and not for government bonds. The client margin for stocks is decided by the investment company. OTC trades for government bonds do not require a margin.

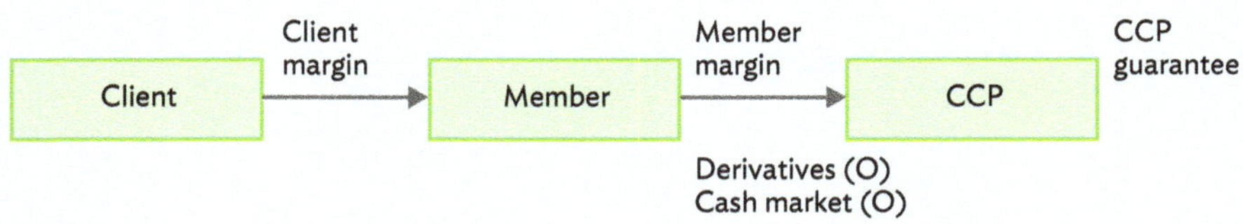


In Japan, for OTC government bonds, the Japan Securities Clearing Corporation calculates the initial margin using a method based on historical price fluctuations. To reflect changes in positions due to intraday DVP settlement, the replacement cost is estimated as the difference between the market value of the original DVP-traded bond and the estimated price after the bidding (assuming insolvency has occurred). In reality, the after-bidding price is estimated based on a reference period of 251 or 501 days, with a confidence level of 99% and a holding period of 3 days. Other charges added to the initial margin include repo rate fluctuation risk and a market impact charge.

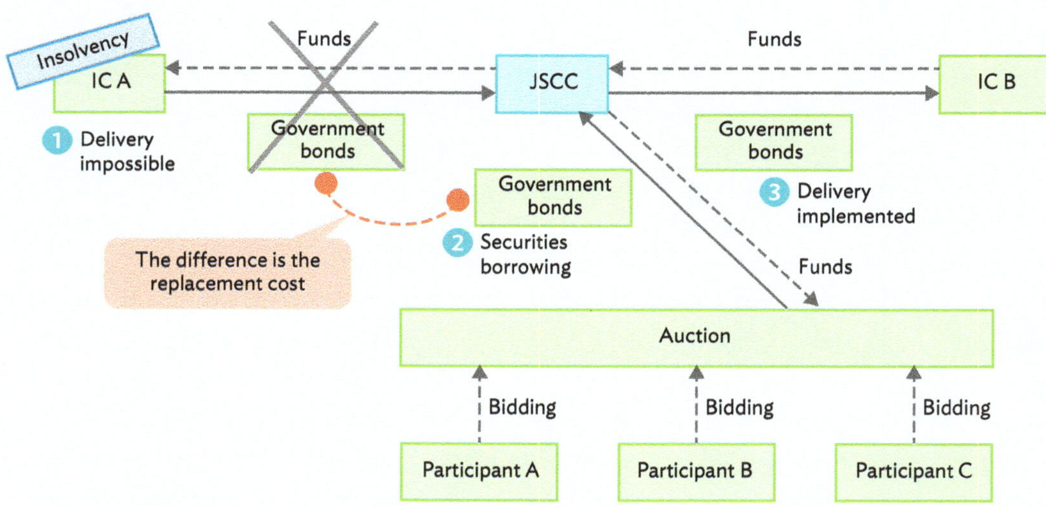


[a] Principles for Financial Market Infrastructures.
JSCC = Japan Securities Clearing Corporation.
Source: JSCC. 2023. *Knowing from Clearing and Settlement JGBs*. Kinzai Institute for Financial Affairs, Inc., p. 186.

## Medium-Term: Recommended Model

In Azerbaijan, over the past decades, both the full prefunding of cash and the moderated settlement agent-guaranteed mechanism have provided practical ways for the carrying out of securities clearing and settlement. The NDC's current clearing function is limited to position calculations among participating financial institutions, and there is no CCP, with the current financial transaction volumes not being very large.

Of particular note, however, if the current guarantee mechanism remains, let us say in DVP1 transactions, the transaction costs could increase, due mainly to the rising cost of the collateral associated with this mechanism. As various emerging economies have experienced, securities trading volume can expand over an unforeseeable period as the economy develops and grows. If a CCP is in place, then the costs are shared among CCP clearing members, and participants can benefit from lower costs, while the available financial resources that participants can utilize become larger.

Therefore, it is recommended that an entity be designated as a CCP and that a CCP risk management framework, including clearing membership and selection of the securities cleared, be established. The CCP should be designated as the mechanism for managing counterparty risk in the securities market to enhance market credibility.[49] In particular, to reduce the restrictiveness of the guarantee mechanism based on trading limit imposition, CCP functionality may help support a larger volume of transactions.

It is advised that a CCP be introduced within a medium-term time frame. Currently, the effectiveness of introducing a CCP might be limited due to low liquidity in securities transactions, but given the resulting enhanced transparency in risk management, it might be considered. To facilitate its introduction, the regulations governing assumption of liabilities, including other relevant rules and agreements, should be reviewed. The decision-making process might include consideration of the clearing of derivative products through a CCP in the future. Securing financial resources for the CCP and building the necessary IT systems will be key parts of the plan.

Since the risks incurred by participating institutions can be transferred to the CCP, the PFMI strongly recommends certain CCP risk management requirements, stating: "the effectiveness of a CCP's risk control and the adequacy of its financial resources are critical to achieving these risk reduction benefits." In this light, in addition to introducing margin arrangements, which is a defaulter's pay scheme, a default fund, which is a survivors' pay scheme, should be established as well.[50] In cases where the defaulted obligations cannot be covered even after the posted collateral is liquidated, the shortfall may be resolved through a sequence of prefunded financial resources (a waterfall).

49 According to PFMI Explanatory Note 3.3.1, a CCP's risk management framework (including policies, procedures, and systems) should enable it to identify, measure, monitor, and effectively manage the range of risks that arise in or are borne by the CCP, and provide appropriate incentives and the relevant information to its participants and other entities to manage and contain risks vis-à-vis the CCP.

50 In Article 58 of the post-trade system of the Law, there is a definition of and requirements for a clearing fund.

A sound CCP clearing structure needs to be discussed among stakeholders, taking into account the Azerbaijani institutional and governance context.[51] A data-dependent approach is needed to select the securities for CCP clearing and to calculate the prefunded default fund amount to be shared among the clearing members.

51 See Committee on Payment and Settlement Systems. 2010. *Market Structure Developments in the Clearing Industry: Implications for Financial Stability*. Bank for International Settlements.

# 5 CONCLUSIONS

Azerbaijan is considering options for the NDC to take on the functions now performed by settlement agents. Based on the research results so far, it is judged that, if the NDC were to assume the settlement guarantee function currently performed by the settlement agents, which are commercial banks, it would face challenges in adequately managing the related settlement risk, due to limitations in its capacity to secure sufficient liquidity. To address this issue, a two-step improvement approach is considered.

As a near-term step, the system design involves relaxing the settlement guarantees of settlement agents. That is, the DVP1 settlement practice is shifted toward having the market participants manage the risks themselves. To alleviate the liquidity burdens resulting from this change, the central bank would consider providing liquidity support. Meanwhile, the existing DVP2 settlement method, requiring sufficient financial pledges, is maintained. Additionally, clearing participants might consider jointly establishing a clearing fund. In the event of a participant's default, liquidity would be supplied from this fund to execute the payment obligations. This approach considers functions similar to those of a CCP default fund and will necessitate the establishment of detailed operational procedures.

As a medium-term step, the NDC will consider functioning as a CCP when agreed upon among relevant stakeholders. For this, the relevant regulations, adequate financial resources, and robust IT system setup are required. This will also involve developing a rigorous risk management framework for the CCP, including a default fund and margin requirements.

The results of the discussion summarized above have yielded Table 5, outlining four recommended actions in the FMI space. In order to strengthen the settlement agent capabilities of the NDC, 12 detailed review agendas for implementing the recommendations in Table 5 have also been derived.

### Table 5: Recommended Actions

| Recommendations | Agency | Timing |
|---|---|---|
| ***Financial market infrastructure*** | | |
| **Design a holistic financial market infrastructure that considers economies of scale, concentration risk management measures, and the Principles for Financial Market Infrastructures.** | | |
| (i) Prepare a robust plan for the implementation of the NDC's sole settlement agent services, including a set of risk management instruments. | NDC | NT |
| (ii) Provide banks and/or investment companies and/or the NDC with a central bank liquidity facility using securities-on-flow as collateral. | CBA | NT |
| (iii) (Subject to fulfillment of Recommendation [ii]) Move away from the "trading limits backed by guarantee requirements" in DVP model 1, if necessary, complementing DVP1 transactions with "margin management." | NDC/Banks/ ICs | MT |
| (iv) Designate an entity as a central counterparty. Establish a central counterparty risk management framework including (a) clearing membership, (b) margins, (c) a default fund, and (d) a waterfall structure. | CBA | MT |

CBA = Central Bank of the Republic of Azerbaijan, DVP = delivery versus payment, IC = investment company, NT = near term (within 1 year), MT = medium term (1~3 years), NDC = National Depository Center.
Source: Asian Development Bank consultants.

The 12 agendas in Table 6 are extracted from the analysis in section IV. It is advised that the CBA and the NDC review these issues further. As the issues discussed are expected to affect the securities clearing and settlement landscape in Azerbaijan, it is necessary to pursue the discussions transparently, in consultation with market participants such as the financial institutions, the BSE, and the other relevant entities. External research, including a detailed empirical impact analysis of CCP clearing, may also be conducted in collaboration with academia.

### Table 6: Detailed Agendas to Supplement Recommended Actions

| | Agendas | Responsible Parties |
|---|---|---|
| (i) | 1. Design account structure, including scheme to link commercial and central bank accounts, and conduct a feasibility study | Market participants (investment companies, banks), BSE, CBA, NDC, etc. |
| | 2. Set up collateral management system, including haircuts based on mark-to-market accounting | |
| | 3. Examine the implementation of margin arrangements | |
| | 4. Upgrade ways of protecting customers' financial pledges in a new environment | |
| | 5. Improve ways of completing final settlement by no later than the end of the value date, and set up a clearing fund | |
| | 6. Improve procedures for monetizing collateral | |
| (ii) | 7. Prepare a scheme for the central bank intraday repo/overdraft provision | CBA |
| | 8. Review policy for access to the central bank account, to accommodate changes in securities market environment | CBA, banks, investment companies, NDC |

*continued on next page*

Table 6 *continued*

| | Agendas | Responsible Parties |
|---|---|---|
| (iii) | 9. Overhaul the existing guarantee mechanism applying to DVP1 transactions | CBA, BSE, banks, investment companies, NDC |
| | 10. Review current and alternate DVP models, including netting effects and ways of expediting intraday settlement effects | |
| | 11. Review trade-related issues, including settlement cycle and securities delivery fails and related arrangements | |
| (iv) | 12. Prepare to introduce CCP functionality, including arrangements for clearing membership, margins, a default fund, and a waterfall scheme | BSE, banks, investment companies, NDC |

BSE = Baku Stock Exchange, CBA = Central Bank of the Republic of Azerbaijan, CCP = central counterparty, DVP = delivery versus payment.
Source: Author.

# GLOSSARY

| Term | Definition |
|---|---|
| **Affiliate** | A company that controls, or is controlled by, or is under common control with, the participant. Control of a company is defined as (i) ownership, control, or holding with power to vote 20% or more of a class of voting securities of the company; or (ii) consolidation of the company for financial reporting purposes. |
| **Assumption of obligation** | The role played by the central counterparty (CCP) in guaranteeing the performance and settlement of trades between market participants. A CCP becomes a counterparty to trades with market participants through novation, or through an analogous legally binding arrangement. Through novation, the original contract between the buyer and the seller is extinguished and replaced by two new contracts—one between the CCP and the buyer and the other between the CCP and the seller. |
| **Book-entry** | The transfer of securities and other financial assets which does not involve the physical movement of paper documents or certificates (for example, the electronic transfer of securities). |
| **Business continuity** | A state of uninterrupted business operations. This term also refers to all of the organizational, technical, and staffing measures used to ensure the continuation of operations following a disruption to a service, including in the event of a wide-scale or major disruption. |
| **Buy-in** | A buy-in by a CCP is a process in which the CCP purchases the securities that a clearing member failed to deliver during settlement. |
| **Cash market** | A cash market for securities is a financial marketplace where investors buy and sell stocks, bonds, and other financial instruments for immediate delivery and payment. The exchange of funds and securities happens simultaneously at the agreed-upon price. |
| **Central bank liquidity facility** | A standing credit facility that can be drawn upon by certain designated account holders (e.g., banks) at the central bank. In some cases, the facility can be used automatically at the initiative of the account holder, while in other cases the central bank may retain some degree of discretion. The loans typically take the form either of advances or overdrafts on an account holder's current account, which may be secured by a pledge of securities or of traditional rediscounting of bills. |
| **Central bank money** | A liability of a central bank, in this case, in the form of deposits held at the central bank, which can be used for settlement purposes. |
| **Central securities depository** | An entity that provides securities accounts, central safekeeping services, and asset services, which may include the administration of corporate actions and redemptions, and which plays an important role in helping to ensure the integrity of securities issues. |
| **Clearing** | The process of transmitting, reconciling, and, in some cases, confirming transactions prior to settlement, potentially including the netting of transactions and the establishment of final positions for settlement. |
| **Close-out liquidation** | The process undertaken by the CCP to liquidate or handle a defaulting participant's positions or obligations. This may involve selling the underlying assets or offsetting positions with other clearing members. |
| **Clearing fund** | A prefunded default arrangement that is composed of assets contributed by a CCP's participants that may be used by the CCP in certain circumstances to cover losses or liquidity pressures resulting from participant defaults. |

| Term | Definition |
| --- | --- |
| **Collateral** | The assets pledged by a borrower to secure a loan or other credit which is subject to seizure in the event of default or a breach of a credit trigger. |
| **Commercial bank money** | A liability of a commercial bank, in the form of deposits held at the commercial bank, which can be used for settlement purposes. |
| **Counterparty** | A party to a trade. |
| **Default** | An event stipulated in an agreement as constituting a default. Generally, such events relate to a failure to complete a transfer of funds or securities in accordance with the terms and rules of the system in question. |
| **Default waterfall** | The sequence for applying a financial market infrastructure's financial resources to losses resulting from a participant's default. |
| **Defaulter pays approach** | Losses from a party's default are borne by the defaulting party through the non-defaulter's liquidation/enforcement of the collateral posted by the defaulting party. |
| **Deferred net settlement** | A net settlement mechanism which settles on a net basis at the end of a predefined settlement cycle. |
| **Delivery versus payment** | A securities settlement mechanism that links a securities transfer and a funds transfer in such a way as to ensure that delivery occurs if and only if the corresponding payment occurs. |
| **Failed transaction** | A transaction that does not settle on the contractual settlement date due to financial, operational, or legal reasons. |
| **General business risk** | Any potential impairment of the financial market infrastructure's financial position (as a business concern) as a consequence of a decline in its revenues or an increase in its expenses, such that expenses exceed revenues and result in a loss that must be charged against capital. |
| **Haircut** | A risk control measure applied to underlying assets whereby the value of those underlying assets is calculated as the market value of the assets reduced by a certain percentage (the "haircut"). Haircuts are applied by a collateral taker in order to protect itself from losses resulting from declines in the market value of a security. |
| **Initial margin** | Collateral that is collected to cover potential changes in the value of each participant's position (that is, potential future exposure) over the appropriate close-out period in the event the participant defaults. |
| **Liquidity covers 1, 2** | Cover 1 refers to the preparation of liquidity for the possible default of the participant and its affiliates with the largest payment obligation, while Cover 2 refers to the case of the default of two participants and their affiliates. |
| **Loss-sharing arrangement** | Rules or other arrangements to allocate losses from a participant's default or other causes. |
| **Margin** | In the context of clearing activity, collateral that is collected to protect against current or potential future exposures resulting from market price changes or in the event of a counterparty default. |
| **Net debit cap** | A limit imposed by a central bank or a clearing organization on the total amount of intraday credit that a participant can utilize in its settlement or clearing account. |
| **Potential future exposure** | Any potential credit exposure that a financial market infrastructure could face at some point in the future. Potential future exposure arises from potential fluctuations in the market value of a participant's open positions between the time they are incurred or reset to the current market price and the time they are liquidated or effectively hedged. |
| **Provision of guarantees** | In Azerbaijan, the guarantees can be provided in the following pre-deposited assets: (i) funds transferred (prefunded cash), (ii) financial pledges, (iii) bank guarantees, and (iv) insurance contracts. |

| Term | Definition |
|---|---|
| **Real-time gross settlement** | The real-time settlement of payments, transfer instructions, or other obligations individually on a transaction-by-transaction basis. |
| **Replacement cost** | The unrealized gain on the unsettled contract or the cost of replacing the original contract at market prices that may be changing rapidly during periods of stress. |
| **Repo** | A contract to sell and subsequently repurchase securities at a specified date and price. |
| **Securities settlement system** | An entity that enables securities to be transferred and settled by book entry according to a set of predetermined multilateral rules. Such systems allow transfers of securities either free of payment or against payment. |
| **Settlement agent** | An institution that manages the settlement process (e.g., the determination of settlement positions, monitoring of the exchange of payments, etc.) for transfer systems or other arrangements that require settlement. In Azerbaijan, a settlement agent is defined as a bank that is a member of the Real-Time Integrated Payment System (Azerbaijan Interbank Payment System) operating in the Republic of Azerbaijan, which determines the trading limits for conducting transactions on the Baku Stock Exchange by investment companies and executes the monetary obligations arising from the transactions concluded by the investment companies in the amounts of those limits. |
| **Settlement asset** | Payments between banks are made by exchanging the liabilities of the settlement institution (the "settlement asset"). The choice of settlement asset in a system—particularly in a system handling large values—is important because of the exposures that can arise between the settlement institution and the participants in the system. |
| **Settlement bank** | An institution that manages the settlement process (e.g., the determination of settlement positions, monitoring of the exchange of payments, etc.) for transfer systems or other arrangements that require settlement. The central bank or a commercial bank can perform this role. |
| **Settlement cycle** | The amount of time that elapses between the trade date (T) and the settlement date (S). Typically measured relative to the trade date, e.g., if 3 days elapse, the settlement interval is T+3. |
| **Settlement risk** | The general term used to designate the risk that settlement in a funds or securities transfer system will not take place as expected. This risk may comprise both credit and liquidity risks. |
| **Survivors' pay** | A principle of loss-sharing arrangements which, in the event of a participant's inability to settle, requires losses to be borne by the surviving participants in accordance with some predetermined formula. |
| **Trading limit** | In Azerbaijan, the monetary limit set by the settlement agent to the investment company for the purchase of securities and derivative financial instruments on the stock exchange during one trading day, including securities subject to repo/counter-repo transactions. A trading limit can be set for the current day, or for a certain future period in advance. |
| **Value date** | The day on which the payment, transfer instruction, or other obligation is due and the associated funds and securities are typically available to the receiving participant. |

Source: CPMI-IOSCO. 2012. *Principles for Financial Market Infrastructures.*

# REFERENCES


Bank of Japan. 2009. *Research Paper: The Bankruptcy of Lehman Brothers and Its Impact on the Japanese Payment System.*

———. 2004. *Functions and Operations of the Bank of Japan. Chapter IV: Payment and Settlement and the Roles of the Bank of Japan.*

Bank of Korea. 2021. *Explanation on Securities Business by the Bank of Korea.*

———. 2023. *Regulation on the Operation and Management of the Payment and Settlement Systems.*

Central Bank of the Republic of Azerbaijan. 2023. *Joint Agreement on Clearing and Settlement of Securities and Derivatives.*

Committee on Payments and Market Infrastructures. 2016. *A Glossary of Terms Used in Payments and Settlement Systems.*

———. 2010. *Market Structure Developments in the Clearing Industry: Implications for Financial Stability.*

Committee on Payments and Market Infrastructures and International Organization of Securities Commissions. 2012. *Principles for Financial Market Infrastructures.*

———. 2012. *Principles for Financial Market Infrastructures: Disclosure Framework and Assessment Methodology.*

Committee on Payments and Settlement Systems. 2003. *The Role of Central Bank Money in Payment Systems.*

Euroclear Bank and Committee on Payments and Market Infrastructures and International Organization of Securities Commissions. 2023. *Euroclear Bank–CPMI-IOSCO Disclosure Framework 2022.*

Japan Securities Clearing Corporation. 2023. *Principles for Financial Market Infrastructures Disclosure.*

Korea Exchange. 2022. *Guide to Korea Exchange Clearing and Settlement.*

National Depository Center. 2019. *Rules of the Post-Trade System and Clearing Activities.*

Republic of Azerbaijan. 2023. *Law On Securities Market.*

Summers, B. 1994. *The Payment System: Design, Management, and Supervision*. International Monetary Fund.

World Bank. 2006. *Payment and Securities Clearance and Settlement Systems in Azerbaijan.*

www.ingramcontent.com/pod-product-compliance
Lightning Source LLC
Chambersburg PA
CBHW041800220926
51847CB00014B/263
*9789292777678*